Dear Andrea,

Congratulations to a GREAT finish to Seminar 2020! I so look forward to working together to continue to support your Dreams!

Love,

Lynn

ADDITIONAL PRAISE FOR *FINISH*

"When it comes to personal achievement, there's a fine line between tragedy and comedy. No one beats Jon Acuff at helping me laugh at my foibles while offering me help to overcome them. If you want to master the art of finishing, read this book!"

—Michael Hyatt, *USA Today* bestselling author of
Living Forward

"Are you haunted by the ghosts of unfinished goals? I never met an idea I didn't like, so I know all about the excitement of starting and the difficulty of finishing. Fortunately, the ever-entertaining Jon Acuff has come to the rescue in this terrific new book. *Finish* identifies the many ways we sabotage our own progress and gives us powerful tools to 'get 'er done.' Read Jon's book, apply its wisdom, and I guarantee you'll cross your personal finish line—laughing all the way."

—Ken Blanchard, coauthor of *The New One Minute Manager*
and *One Minute Mentoring*

"Jon Acuff is speaking the preferred language of all great leaders: get things done! If you want to stand out today, then it's imperative for you to be a finisher, and Jon has provided a practical, inspiring, and seamless roadmap for moving things across the finish line. *Finish* is an instant classic!"

—Brad Lomenick, author of *H3 Leadership*

"When you're a leader, one of your biggest hopes is that your team will finish its goals. But with thousands of distractions, it gets harder and harder every year. This book goes a long way to help fix that problem. I predict that organizations will buy this by the box!"

—Reggie Joiner, CEO and founder of The reThink Group

"As a musician and now pastor, I know the challenges of writing songs and sermons. This book shows us all not only how to finish, but how to finish *well*. My friend Jon has a way of making the impossible seem practical."

—Montell Jordan, author of *This is How We Do It!*

"As an author, I know how challenging it is to finish. That last chapter is always a challenge, but the tips Jon provides in his new book make it a lot easier. If you've got something you want done, read this book!"

—Andy Andrews, *New York Times* bestselling author of *The Traveler's Gift* and *The Noticer*

"*Finish* is the ultimate kick-in-the-pants you always knew you needed."

—Claire Díaz-Ortiz, author and entrepreneur, ClaireDiazOrtiz.com

FINISH

FINISH

GIVE YOURSELF THE GIFT OF DONE

Jon Acuff

PORTFOLIO / PENGUIN

Portfolio / Penguin
An imprint of Penguin Random House LLC
375 Hudson Street
New York, New York 10014
penguin.com

Copyright © 2017 by Jonathan Acuff

Most Portfolio books are available at a discount when purchased in quantity for sales promotions or corporate use. Special editions, which include personalized covers, excerpts, and corporate imprints, can be created when purchased in large quantities. For more information, please call (212) 572-2232 or e-mail specialmarkets@penguinrandomhouse.com. Your local bookstore can also assist with discounted bulk purchases using the Penguin Random House corporate Business-to-Business program. For assistance in locating a participating retailer, e-mail B2B@penguinrandomhouse.com.

Some names and details were changed to protect the privacy of the individuals in each story.

Library of Congress Cataloging-in-Publication Data Available
ISBN: 9781591847625
9780698184800 (EL)
9780525533313 (Exp)

Printed in the United States of America
7   9   10   8   6

Book design by Daniel Lagin

For my parents, Mark and Libby Acuff,
who believed I was a writer long before I did.

CONTENTS

CONTENTS

FINISH

INTRODUCTION

The Wrong Ghost

I fought the wrong ghost in 2013.

That year, I published a book urging readers to start. I challenged them to get off the couch. I dared people to launch a business. I encouraged them to begin a diet or a write a book or pursue a million other goals they'd been dreaming about for years.

I thought the biggest problem for people was the phantom of fear that prevented them from beginning. If I could just nudge them across the starting line, everything would work out. Fear was the ghost holding them back and starting was the only way to beat it.

I was half right.

The start does matter. The beginning is significant. The first few steps are critical, but they aren't the most important.

Do you know what matters more? Do you know what makes the start look silly and easy and almost insignificant?

The finish.

Year after year, readers have pulled me aside at events and said, "I've never had a problem starting. I've started a million things, but I never finish them. How do I finish?"

I didn't have an answer, but I needed one in my own life, too.

I've finished a few things. I've run half marathons, written six books, and dressed myself pretty well today, but those are the exceptions in my half-done life.

I've only completed 10 percent of the books I own. It took me three years to finish six days of the P90X home exercise program. When I was twenty-three I made it to blue belt in karate, approximately seventy-six belts below finishing the goal of black belt. I have thirty-two half-started Moleskine notebooks in my office and nineteen tubes of nearly finished Chapstick in my bathroom. A financial adviser would probably go bananas over the hydrated lips category of my personal budget.

My garage is also a mausoleum to almost. There's the telescope (used five times), the fishing pole (used three times), and the snowboard with a season pass to a local mountain (used zero times). And who can forget the moped I bought three years ago and rode a total of twenty-two miles! I didn't even title or register it. I live off the grid. The grid of done.

At least I'm not alone in my unfinishing ways.

According to studies, 92 percent of New Year's resolutions fail. Every January, people start with hope and hype, believing that this will be the New Year that does indeed deliver a New You.

But though 100 percent start, only 8 percent finish. Statistically you've got the same shot at getting into Juilliard to become a ballerina as you do at finishing your goals. Their acceptance rate is about 8 percent, tiny dancer.

I thought my problem was that I didn't try hard enough. That's what every shiny-toothed guru online says. "You've got to hustle! You must grind! Sleep when you're dead!"

Maybe I was just lazy.

After all, I knew that I had dangerously low levels of "grit" in my life. I learned that when I measured myself on Angela Duckworth's excellent "Grit Scale." My score was so low that it didn't even make the chart. There should have been bonus points for finishing the test, which I surprisingly did.

I started getting up earlier. I drank enough energy drinks to kill a horse. I hired a life coach and ate more superfoods.

Nothing worked, although I did develop a pretty nice eyelid tremor from all the caffeine. It was as if my eye were waving at you, very, very quickly.

While I was busy putting elbow grease on the grindstone and reaching for the stars like Abe Lincoln, I created a 30-day challenge online. It was called the 30 Days of Hustle, and it was a video course that helped thousands of people knock out their goals.

What happened next was at best an accident. You're not supposed to admit that in books like this. When you write self-help tomes, it's tempting to rewrite your own past as proof that you are qualified to help someone else's future.

The leader who stumbled into success goes back in time and invents ten steps that got him there so that he can write a book called *10 Steps That Will Get You There*. I honestly didn't plan what I'm about to tell you. I was as surprised as you are going to be. If anything, I'm just excited it actually worked.

In the spring of 2016, a researcher from the University of Memphis named Mike Peasley approached me with a proposition.

He wanted to study people who took my 30 Days of Hustle goal-setting course to analyze what worked and what didn't. He was finishing his PhD and wanted to write papers about what his study revealed. In the months that followed, he surveyed more than 850 participants to build a solid foundation of real data.

This was a new experience for me, because prior to that I was operating under the great "Make Up Whatever You Want to Say on the Internet with No Foundation in Fact" ordinance of 2003.

What he learned changed my entire approach to finishing, to this book, and in some ways, to my life.

Mike found that people who completed the course had a 27 percent greater chance of success over other times they had attempted goal setting. That was encouraging but not really surprising, given that when you work on something consistently for thirty days, you get better at it.

What was astonishing to me is something that should be more apparent to all of us: the exercises that caused people to increase their progress dramatically were those that took the pressure off, those that did away with the crippling perfectionism that caused people to quit their goals. Whether they were trying to lose a pants size, write more content on a blog, or get a raise, the results were the same. The less that people aimed for perfect, the more productive they became.

It turns out that trying harder isn't the answer.

Grinding more isn't the solution.

Chronic starters can become consistent finishers.

We can finish.

Admit it, you felt like this book was going to be similar to a Red Bull commercial. I'd give you a few tips, get you motivated, show you how to get the eye of the tiger, and help you do more, more, more!

How's that working out for you? Is trying harder helping? Is doing more making you like life more? Have any of the productivity tips, time management tricks, or life hacks helped even a little bit?

They haven't and they won't.

If you want to finish, you've got to do all that you can to get rid of your perfectionism right out of the gate. You've got to have fun, cut your goal in half, choose what things you'll bomb, and a few other actions you won't see coming at first.

That's what was surprising about this whole adventure. The practical lessons the research taught me about what it takes to really finish are so counterintuitive that most of them will feel like shortcuts. You'll feel like you're cheating or that what you're doing "doesn't count."

Do you feel a little guilty about the word "shortcut"? Are you remembering every coach, boss, or parent who told you, "There are no shortcuts in life"?

Fine, just promise me you'll stop using Google. Next time you need to know something, write the Library of Congress a letter.

On paper. With a stamp you have to lick with your naked tongue. Those sticker stamps are a shortcut.

That's essentially what the Wright Brothers had to do in order to find somewhere to test their planes. They wrote the U.S. Weather Bureau in Washington, D.C., and asked where the best wind in the country was. A bureaucrat did some research, pulled together reports, and then wrote them back. After they pored over the data, they picked Kitty Hawk, North Carolina. Next, they wrote the postmaster there to inquire about what the island was really like. Then they waited for his response.

The process took forever, at least by our standards today, because now we've got shortcuts.

Asking a Martha's Vineyard local for a beach recommendation is a shortcut. (The answer is "go to Tashmoo," by the way.)

Turning Wi-Fi off on your laptop when you need to focus on something is a shortcut.

Refusing to keep ice cream in your house when you're trying to lose weight is a shortcut.

If you're tired of starting and not finishing, I've got a few things to show you. And it all begins with how you deal with the most important day of any goal.

CHAPTER 1

The Day After Perfect

"Well begun is half done" is one of my favorite false motivational statements. The other is "Sometimes you have to jump off the cliff and grow your wings on the way down." I saw that one on a photo of a wolf, which was puzzling because in my limited understanding of the animal kingdom, no wolf has ever grown wings. Thank goodness they haven't. If wolves ever figure out the mechanics of flight, it's game over.

We tend to put too much emphasis on beginnings. In doing so, we miss the single day that wrecks more goals than any other. For the first forty-one years of my life I didn't even hear anyone mention this day. I was as clueless as the fictitious people who still live at the beach where *Jaws* was filmed. There shouldn't have been a *Jaws 2*. That movie should have just been called *A Bunch of Seaside Residents Move to Ohio, Where There Are No Sharks*. That's probably not going to fit on a marquee, but at least they would have avoided another shark-related disaster.

Despite all the work we put into planning our goals, despite the new sneakers and diets and business plans, we miss the day that matters most, the day that is why I'm not allowed to buy black beans at Costco anymore.

The store will let me, it's not a management decision, although I do abuse those free samples. One day they were giving out Oreos, for the seven Americans who have never experienced that cookie. The conversation with the employee handing them out was awkward because I felt like I had to pretend I'd never heard of them. "What do you call this? A chocolate cookie sandwich? No? The name is 'Oreo'? Am I saying that correctly? How whimsical!"

The reason I can't buy black beans is that they only sell them in pallet quantity. You can't just buy one, you have to buy a thousand cans.

That's a lot of beans, but at least once a year I believe I need this amount.

While exercising, I decide to "get serious." I remember that in Timothy Ferriss's book *The 4-Hour Body,* he recommends a simple breakfast of eggs, black beans, spinach, cumin, and salsa. When my family sees me rooting around the cupboard for black beans, they all groan. "Oh no, here we go again."

They know that for the next twelve days in a row I am going to eat black beans.

Why only twelve? Because on Day 13 I'm going to get too busy, have a meeting, or be on a business trip without my traveling beans. Upon missing one day, I will quit the whole endeavor.

Once the streak is broken, I can't pick it back up. My record is no longer perfect so I quit altogether. This is a surprisingly common reaction to mistakes.

If you interview people about why they quit their goals, they all use similar language.

"I fell behind and couldn't get back on track."

"Life got in the way and my plans got derailed."

"The project jumped the tracks and got too messy to fix."

The words might be different, but they're all saying the redundant same thing: "When it stopped being perfect, I stopped, too."

You missed one day of your diet and then decided the whole thing was dumb.

You were too busy to write one morning and so you put your unfinished book back on the shelf.

You lost one receipt and then gave up on your entire budget for the month.

I'm not picking on you for giving in to perfectionism. I've fallen to it many times as well. One February, I ran seventy-five miles. Then I ran seventy-one in March and seventy-three in April. Know how much I ran in May? Eight miles. Can you guess June's total? Three.

Why? Because when my perfect exercise streak hit a road-block I stopped.

This is the first lie that perfectionism tells you about goals: Quit if it isn't perfect.

The genius in this first lie is subtle. It's not "when" it isn't perfect, because that hints at the reality that it won't be. No,

FINISH

perfectionism tells you "if" it isn't perfect, as if you have the chance to run the whole rack and go to the grave with a 100 percent on your tombstone.

This is troubling to us, because we don't want B's and C's when we've got a goal. We want straight A's, especially if it's a goal we've thought about for any amount of time. We will gladly give up the whole thing when we discover some error or imperfection in our performance. More than that, we will even prequit, before we've even begun.

That's why a lot of people won't start a new goal. They'd rather get a zero than a fifty. They believe perfect is the only standard, and if they can't hit it they won't even take the first step. A dreary sense of "What's the use?" settles about them like a thick fog. I can't fail if I don't try.

While researching this book, I asked a thousand people in an online poll if they had ever refused to even write down an idea because they judged it as not good enough. I thought maybe I was the only one who had a perfectionism filter that sorted ideas before they were allowed to hit a piece of paper. More than 97 percent of the participants said they had done that.

I don't know how to tell you this, but your goal will not be perfect. It crushes me to break this to you, but you will fail. Maybe a lot. Maybe right out of the gate. You might even trip over the starting line.

That's OK.

Why? Why would I encourage you to embrace imperfection? Well, for one thing, doing something imperfectly won't kill you.

10

We think it will, which is why we compare our lack of progress to a train crash. "I couldn't get back on track, my plans got derailed." A train derailment is a significant, serious accident. In many cases, people die, hundreds of thousands of dollars in damage occurs, and fixing it takes days if not weeks.

Do you know what doesn't happen when you miss a day of your goal? Any of those things.

No one dies. It doesn't require $400,000 to get back on track. Righting things doesn't take four weeks.

Second, developing tolerance for imperfection is the key factor in turning chronic starters into consistent finishers. Chronic starters quit the day after perfect. What's the use? The streak is over. Better to wallow in the mistake. I ate a crazy dinner last night, might as well eat a crazy breakfast, lunch, and dinner today, too.

"Might as well" is one of the most dangerous phrases in the English language. Or Polish, since for some reason my books tend to get translated into that language before Spanish. I am killing it in Krakow.

"Might as well" is never applied to good things. It's never, "Might as well help all these orphans," or "Might as well plant something healthy in this community garden." It's usually the white flag of surrender. "I've had a single French fry, might as well eat a thousand."

These are the kinds of things we say on the day after perfect, and that day is sticky.

Do you know the biggest day for people to drop out of the 30

Days of Hustle goal-setting course? Most people guess Day 23 or Day 15, but that's not even close.

Day 2 is when I see the largest drop-off. That's right, the biggest day for the most people to stop opening the e-mails that constitute the exercises is Day 2. Why that day? Because imperfection doesn't take long to show up. You've sat at your desk on a Monday morning before and thought, "It's nine A.M. How am I already this far behind? How is this entire week already ruined?"

Imperfection is fast, and when it arrives we usually quit.

That's why the day after perfect is so important.

This is the make-or-break day for every goal. This is the day after you skipped the jog. This is the day after you failed to get up early. This is the day after you decided the serving size for a whole box of Krispy Kreme Doughnuts is one.

The day after perfect is what separates finishers from starters.

Accomplishing a goal is a lot less like taking a train across country and a lot more like driving a bumper car. Some days, you will circle the track without a single impediment. Nothing will stand in your way, and for a few brief moments that bumper car will actually feel fast. On other days, some completely unforeseen, impossible-to-account-for situation is going to slam into your side. Or you'll get locked into a really annoying cluster of other cars and feel like you've taken five steps back.

This is going to happen.

You will not be perfect, but do you know what's even more important than perfection? Do you know what will serve you far longer than perfectionism ever could?

Moving forward imperfectly.

Reject the idea that the day after perfect means you've failed.

That's just not true.

You get to try again.

Today, tomorrow, next week.

Unfortunately, perfectionism dies slowly. It's persistent and particularly dangerous because it masquerades as excellence. Some readers have already felt uncomfortable with this chapter because they think the opposite of perfectionism is failure. It's not. The opposite is finished.

Those are the doors we stand before in this book and in our lives. One is marked FINISHED and leads to untold adventures, opportunities, and stories. One is marked PERFECTIONISM and leads to a solid brick wall of frustration, shame, and incomplete hopes.

The worst part of this whole situation is that starting goals and never completing them feels terrible.

When you make a goal, you make a promise to yourself. You're going to lose a few pounds. You're going to declutter a closet. You're going to start a blog. You're going to call an old friend. The moment you create that goal, you've made a silent promise. When you don't finish it, you've broken that promise. You've lied to the person you spend the most time with. You.

If you break enough promises, you start to doubt yourself. This is not surprising. If someone told you a dozen different times that they'd meet you for coffee and they didn't show every time, you wouldn't trust them. If a parent promised to pick you up after soccer practice and then didn't, you'd lose faith in him. If a boss promised you a promotion and then didn't deliver month after month, you'd quit believing her.

Why do so many people quit their New Year's resolutions? Because they quit last year and the year before that and the year before that. If you quit enough times, quitting is no longer just a possibility when you start a new goal, it's your identity, and that feels terrible.

People remember uncompleted goals better than completed ones. Your inability to let something go, that feeling that something unfinished is gnawing at you, isn't just a feeling. It's a scratch in the record, a pothole in the road, a never forgotten reminder of a loop you did not close. That's what happens to all of us when we make goals and then have them interrupted by life.

Conversely, finishing something you care about is the best feeling in the world. Starting definitely delivers a momentary burst of euphoria, but it's nothing in comparison to the real finish. You'll keep the medal you received when you finished your first 5K. You don't even care about how long the race took. You did it. You crossed that finish line and every day of training was worth it. Your diploma, the first dollar earned at a business you founded, the business card that says "partner"—small or big, the size of the finish doesn't matter. You finished and that's an amazing feeling.

The problem is that perfectionism magnifies your mistakes and minimizes your progress. It does not believe in incremental

THE DAY AFTER PERFECT

success. Perfectionism portrays your goal as a house of cards. If one thing doesn't go perfectly, the whole thing falls apart. The smallest misstep means the entire goal is ruined.

Perfectionism also messes us up by making us aim too high. There are perhaps a thousand reasons 92 percent of resolutions fail, but one of the greatest is also one of the most deceptive.

When we create a goal, we aim for something better. We want to look better. We want to feel better. We want to be better. But then better turns into best. We don't want small growth. We want massive, overnight success.

Who wants to run a 5K when you can run a marathon? Who wants to write the outline for a book when you can write a three-part trilogy with space werewolf zombies who are in love? (Title: *Full Moon, Full Heart.*) Who wants to make $10,000 when you can make $100,000?

While searching for real examples, from real people, I asked friends on Facebook about perfectionism. One person described it this way: "I start with the belief that I could do something. Then I get all excited and start dreaming. At first I feel confident and like I know what I am doing. Then my dreams get big. Then I want perfection. Then all of a sudden I feel inadequate to do the job because I don't know how to do it at that level. Then the dreams die and the goal is forgotten. The best part is most of the time all that I mentioned above is mental. I never actually started anything."

If you're not naturally tempted to think this way, most of our "chase your dreams, accomplish your goals" literature will push you in this direction.

A fellow motivational author encourages readers to visualize "a movie of you doing perfectly whatever it is that you want to do better." There's that word "perfectly." You're supposed to watch an imaginary movie of yourself doing something perfectly over and over again. At one point, you even crawl inside the movie to really get the sense of perfection. After watching your movie, you're instructed to shrink the image "down to the size of a cracker."

The first time I read that bit of instruction, that I was supposed to turn my goal into a fictional perfect cracker, I started laughing out loud at my desk. I had a sense of where this instruction was going and I was not to be disappointed.

"Then, bring this miniature screen up to your mouth, chew it up and swallow it."

If you ever wonder why you have a hard time with motivational advice, please refer to the dream cracker you were supposed to eat as a way to accomplish your goal.

The harder you try to be perfect, the less likely you'll accomplish your goals.

I know that feels backward, but that's what the research says over and over again.

I wish that were enough to quiet that ever-present demon, but perfectionism is not so easily vanquished. It's far more persistent than that. It digs deeper into our subconscious and is not so easily removed.

Throughout this book, we will return to perfectionism as our ultimate villain.

Perfectionism will do its best to knock you down when you work on a goal. At every turn, it will kick you in the shins, steal your lunch money, and fill you with doubt.

How do I know? Because that's what it does to me and everyone I know who tries.

That's OK, though, because we know something most people don't.

Day 1 isn't the most important day of a goal.

The day after perfect is, and now we're ready for it.

It will be painful and uncomfortable sometimes, but if you learn to stand this minor discomfort, you'll be able to power past the day after perfect. You'll be able to keep your word to yourself. And you'll be able to finish.

CHAPTER 2

Cut Your Goal in Half

When I was a freshman in college, I wanted to try out for the football team. Given my 5'7" soft frame, this makes complete sense. You can't keep a tiger out of the jungle.

I decided to become a field-goal kicker. I bought a stand and a football at a sporting goods store. Late at night, I'd sneak into the stadium in Birmingham, Alabama, and practice my kicks.

Had I ever kicked a field goal? No. Had I ever played a single down of football? No. Did I ever make a field goal during my private midnight practices? Also, no.

So then why did I think I could walk on as a field-goal kicker for a Division I college team that occasionally played schools like Auburn?

Because I am crazy.

That was a foolish goal.

You're not as foolhardy as me, but you probably tend to overreach a bit with your goals, too.

We all supersize our goals at the beginning and the reason why is simple.

Perfectionism.

In the middle of a goal, perfectionism gets real chatty. The first thing it says is that you won't be able to do something perfectly and you shouldn't even start. Far better to give up now than waste all that time and fail.

Perfectionism trots out a laundry list of reasons you shouldn't begin. You're too old. You're too young. You're too busy. You have too many goals and don't know which one to focus on. You don't have enough money or support. Someone else has already done the exact thing you want to do. Someone smarter with better teeth.

If you ignore this initial barrage and start something, perfectionism changes its tune completely. Now it says that you have to do it perfectly. It's the only possibility that is acceptable.

What's brilliant about that "do it perfectly" tactic is that it seems logical. If you are going to do something, shouldn't it be amazing? Shouldn't it be larger than life?

Go big or go home!

We've now bumped into the second lie of perfectionism: Your goal should be bigger.

That's a fun sentiment, and the bigger the goal, the bigger the initial rush we get from imagining it, but today I'm going to dare you to do the opposite. In fact, I want you to cut your goal in half.

I'm not telling you to do less—doing this will actually help you do more.

Think about it this way. At the beginning, when our excitement is through the roof, we think our achievement must be as well. This is why people who have never run one hundred yards will tell me they are going to run a marathon. I will gently ask them, "Have you ever run a half marathon? Have you ever run a 5K? What about a K? Have you ever run just a single K? Get yourself a tiny little medal?"

The answer is always no, they've never run before, but they insist on doing that marathon.

Have you ever wondered why 92 percent of people fail at their goals?

Because we tend to set goals that are foolishly optimistic.

Scientists call this "planning fallacy," a concept first studied by Daniel Kahneman and Amos Tversky. They described this problem as "a phenomenon in which predictions about how much time will be needed to complete a future task display an optimism bias and underestimate the time needed."

Study after study has confirmed that we are prone to fall prey to planning fallacy, but one of my favorite examples involved college seniors working on honors theses.

Psychologist Roger Buehler asked the students to predict how long it would take to finish their theses, with both best-case and worst-case scenarios. On average, the students guessed it would take thirty-four days to finish. In reality, it took them fifty-six days, almost twice as long.

What's really interesting is that not even half the students finished by their worst-case estimate. Even estimating that everything that could go wrong did, the students didn't guess correctly.

Across every form of goal setting, you see planning fallacy rear its ugly head. When he was twenty-three, a friend of mine decided to try something big. He hadn't run anywhere except on a treadmill or during a pickup soccer game. He barely swam a few laps at a pool once or twice a month. He hadn't ridden a bike except the stationary one at the gym. What did he decide to do in that moment? The next 70.3-mile Ironman in San Antonio, Texas.

"I had eight months to train so I went to work on planning out my regimen. I was already going to the gym every weekday so it would be easy to spend more time on running/swimming/biking than on lifting, right? I planned it out, had it all ready to go. And never went to the gym again."

What's amazing about that is the goal wrecked what he was already doing. Before that massive goal showed up, he was consistently going to the gym. Not only did he not do the race, he quit everything that was already in motion. That's how powerfully destructive a wrong-sized goal is.

This goes against every sappy motivational statement in that cursive script on photos of a waterfall universe, but if you dream too big at the start, you curse your finish.

That's certainly what the data will tell you.

On Day 9 of my 30 Days of Hustle program, I asked participants to cut their goals in half, just like I'm asking you. My theory was that people, especially chronic starters like you and me, overestimate what they can accomplish in a set period of time. When they fail to hit the massive goal, it leads to discouragement, which results in people quitting and never finishing.

For instance, if your goal was to lose ten pounds and you lost only eight, you would have failed by two pounds. Most of us believe the old adage, "Shoot for the moon. Even if you miss, you'll land among the stars," but that's not how life really works. The all-or-nothing mentality of perfectionism tells us that close doesn't count. The stars are not good enough.

You now have an ocean of incentive to quit your goal. But if you'd cut the goal in half to five pounds and then lost eight, you'd be a lot more likely to continue because of your initial victory. You would have lost the same amount of weight, but one approach would have almost guaranteed that you'd finish your initial goal and try another one.

"Cut your goal in half" is not the kind of thing you'd see painted on the wall of a gym. It felt like a cheat, but it worked.

When my researcher sent me his report on the 30 Days of Hustle, one result stood out: Those who cut their goal in half increased their performance from past similar goal-related challenges on average by over 63 percent.

Not only that, 90 percent of the people who cut their goal in half said they had an increased desire to work on their goal; it encouraged them to keep going, and it motivated them to work harder because the goal seemed attainable.

The people who took the shortcut finished.

But don't take my word for it. Here are real people just like you who tried this approach.

> I wrote 30 new blog posts of 300+ words each day on my blog. I cut my goal in half to write 100+ words each day. And I did WERK. 28 out of 30 days I wrote 300+ words on my blog, the other 2 days I wrote 100+words. The goal was to write, and write I did!

> I bite off more than I can chew, always. I am glad you cut the goal in ½. My goal was "re-organized" about 4 times because it is demanding a lot of time that was not available. SO, although I didn't attain my original goal, I am further down the field than I would have been a month ago. I am starting the hustle on the next phase of my goal and I now feel like I have the tools to apply with some thought.

> I lost 6 lbs.! Was hoping for 10, but since I cut my goal in half, I met and exceeded it! Here's to another 30 days!

Do you see what happened in each of these cases? They cut their goals in half, still did great, and, most important, are eager to do it again. That's the key. Most people will think this approach is weak, but hard-core approaches that force you to over-reach forget to take in the importance of the word "pace."

Goals are a marathon, not a sprint. I know that if I can get you to do a little one month and win, you're more likely to do a little more the next month and win even more. In the course of a year or maybe even a lifetime that approach will always beat the kill-yourself-for-a-month approach. That tends to end one of two ways: you miss your goal and give up, or you hit your goal and are so spent that you give up.

No, for me the best sign that a paced approach can work is the very last thing the last person above said: "Here's to another 30 days!"

What if You Can't Cut It in Half?

What if you have to pay down $50,000 in credit card debt? What if that's your goal and the thought of cutting that number in half and only paying $25,000 makes you want to throw up a little? Or a lot.

Some goals are difficult to cut in half. For those, don't cut them in half; give yourself more time. If you doubled the amount of time you gave yourself to pay off the debt, what's the worst thing that would happen? You'd pay a little more in interest but you'd still pay off the whole debt. Remember, we're up against quitting. The options we're talking about right now aren't: 1. Finish perfectly, or 2. Cut the goal in half. Those aren't the choices we're debating. The options are: 1. Quit the goal because it was too big, or 2. Cut it in half and finish it.

I'm trying to keep you out of the 92 percent who fail.

And if that means extending your timeline, then you should.

Those two approaches, cutting the goal in half or doubling the timeline, can be applied to most goals.

Obviously, if your goal is to take medicine or something life-saving, by all means do not cut that in half. Or if it's to not punch coworkers in the face, don't start punching half as many as you desire. If you're training for a race and have a very regimented training plan, respect that. A race plan doesn't fit into this idea, because your measured plan created by an expert already prevents you from having a goal that is too big.

How Does the Half-Off Rule Impact Work Goals?

If you have some goals at work that your boss gave you, there's a chance the "cut your goal in half" idea won't work. It's unrealistic to think that you have the power to just cut all your annual goals in half. I agree. But when it comes to corporate goals you don't have control over, the research suggesting that reduced goals perform better over the long run gives you ammunition to set the right goal in the first place.

I once worked at a company that took twenty years to make a $5 million annual revenue on the back of one great product. The CEO decided one year that the company's new goal was to make another $5 million in five years on a brand-new, untested product. Everyone smiled when she announced this aggressive new initiative in the boardroom, but the break room tends to tell the truth about a company.

Everyone knew it was impossible—not just out of reach, but irresponsible in its overreach. It would demand resources, distract us from our real goals, and ultimately fizzle out with a whimper. That's exactly what happened. After a frustrating year, the goal was tweaked, changed, and eventually abandoned.

Few things demoralize a workforce like a leader who doesn't pick the right-sized goal. If you think it's discouraging to break a promise to yourself, imagine multiplying that discouragement by a hundred or even a thousand employees.

How do you apply the 50 percent rule to work goals? By making sure they're the right size from the beginning. How do you do that though? That's what the rest of the book is about, but chapter 7 in particular will be important for work goals. Pulling data from the past will inform the planning of goals in the future. The bottom line in corporate settings is that even if you can't cut a goal in half, you can help temper dangerous optimism and planning fallacy in your company.

It's Almost Never Now or Never

When you're fighting a foe, there are two approaches—defense and offense. Defense is coming up with a plan for when you're attacked. Offense is attacking first.

In the last chapter, we went on defense and prepared for the inevitable day after perfect. We knew it was coming and wanted to be ready. In this chapter, we went on offense and decided to cut our goal in half right out of the gate.

If you still don't want to, I dare you to do a simple exercise. Ask yourself, "What's the worst that could happen?"

Let's pretend for a minute that you cut your goal in half and instead of cleaning your entire house, you cleaned just two rooms. For years, you've hated how cluttered your house is and the idea of doing only two rooms doesn't seem like enough.

What's interesting about this moment is that perfectionism will now tell you that you can do it quickly. Do you see how often it changes tactics depending on the situation? Remember, at the beginning of a goal it tells you that you'll never be able to do something. Now, it's telling you to do it perfectly and quickly.

What if you doubled the timeline instead of cutting the goal in half? If you've had a messy house for five years, why is giving yourself an extra month to clean it so terrifying? You've waited sixty months to do anything and now it has to be done this month?

Perfectionism will tell you it's now or never, forever obsessed with the idea that if you don't finish it now, you never will. Most New Year's resolutions are actually January resolutions. We're so eager to have an amazing month that we exhaust ourselves in the first three weeks of the year and never make it to February. That's just perfectionism trying to puppet-master your timeline.

So, what's the worst that would happen if you cut your goal in half or gave yourself more time? We already know the best that could happen. You'd improve your odds of success by 63 percent. But would the world fall apart if you did less or it took longer?

This idea definitely goes against every goal-setting bit of wisdom you've ever heard. I know that, but remember, we're trying to do two things here: 1. Finish. 2. Beat perfectionism.

And perfectionism absolutely hates this chapter. Cutting your goal in half is Kryptonite for perfectionism. It makes absolutely no sense and sends a bright flare into the night about your intentions. Not only are you refusing to give in to perfectionism, you're setting yourself up for success before you've even started.

I know it's weird, I really do, and you've never done it before. But unless you want the same old results, you'll have to do a few new things.

Start by cutting that goal in half.

Actions:

1. Think back to other goals you've attempted. Were they too big? Write down what happened.

2. Write down a number associated with your goal. (It's difficult to cut a feeling in half.) Will you read ten books? Declutter four rooms? Lose twenty pounds? Make five thousand dollars?

3. Decide whether you can cut your goal in half or double the timeline.

4. Share your goal with someone you trust and ask him if it's too extreme.

5. If you're uncomfortable with cutting your goal in half, spend a few minutes answering the question "What's the worst that could happen?"

CHAPTER 3

Choose What to Bomb

"I'm really excited because I'll be able to demonstrate our full range of capabilities on your lawn."

This is yard-guy speak for "You have the worst grass ever," and it was what I was told when we lived in Atlanta.

From a distance, our lawn looked green. From up close, though, you could quickly see that if you removed every weed I'd be left with a naked patch of red Georgia clay. We were dealing with a 10-to-1 weed-to-grass ratio, and the yard guy smiled with abandon as he stood in our driveway.

He knew that he'd get to sell us a dozen different services with names even more chemical sounding than "Hydrox cookies." He might even find a new species of weed they would name after him, like some suburban botanist. I didn't have a yard, I had a weed laboratory.

I think husbands are supposed to feel ashamed about that. It's bad enough that handymen who come over to our house talk to my wife, Jenny, since she has a degree in construction management, while I have delicate, callus-free writer fingers. I also once threw my car rim and flat tire down the side of a mountain because I was mad at the state of North Carolina. I didn't know you were supposed to keep the rim, which is something they probably teach you in Boy Scouts. All those things are bad, but the yard is the worst. It's a reflection of your manhood and something you talk about while grunting next to a grill with another guy in your neighborhood.

"You put down some new sod? Looks great, Mitch. What's that you say? Sorry, I can't hear you over this gas-powered chain saw I keep running at all times in case I need to do some impromptu logging. Didn't mean to say 'impromptu.' That sounds a little too French for me."

I didn't care that my yard was something best navigated by Dr. Livingstone, I presume. It could have been on fire and I wouldn't have minded one bit.

Why?

Because I had two toddlers at the time.

Kids are a crisis. They're a beautiful crisis, but they're a crisis nonetheless. No one tells you this because they want you to have kids, too, so that the species survives. You don't realize it when you're in the middle of it either. Your only goal is to crawl across the finish line of an early bedtime and live to see another day. "Dad, the sun's still out and I can hear other kids playing." "I don't care, it's bedtime."

Older kids aren't necessarily easier. My eleven-year-old daughter told me one night that when I die, she's going to live off my dead fund. "Do you mean life insurance?" I asked. "Sure, whatever," she replied. At least you can reason with an elementary school student, though.

Toddlers are relentless. You ever have your baby put her hand in the oven? No? Just me? Gotcha. Your yard is the least of your concerns. Who has time to figure out the sprinkler pattern Bermuda grass enjoys versus fescue? You're on high alert, riding the wave back down from a toddler meltdown or building back toward one because the chicken strips you served today were the wrong shape. They were the right shape yesterday. They were the only acceptable shape, but today oblong is cause for panic and so you find yourself digging elbow deep in a bag of chicken strips you used to malign other parents for feeding their kids, looking for the magical bit of pressed chicken that will end this struggle.

Grass doesn't matter.

It might later. When you're out of the toddler zone you'll have time for things like your yard and pants that aren't of the sweat variety, but for now, you better practice choosing what to bomb.

The only way to accomplish a new goal is to feed it your most valuable resource: time. And what we never like to admit is that you don't just give time to something, you take it from something else. To be good at one thing you have to be bad at something else.

Perfectionism's third lie is: You can do it all. I'm here to tell you that you can't.

You know this deep down, but there's still a part of you, a

part run by shame, that thinks you're one or two apps away from doing it all. This is why chronic starters are always reading books about time management. Perhaps if we sliced the day just a little differently or combined an audiobook with the treadmill while also flossing, we could manage to get it all done.

I'm here today to tell you that you can't get it all done. Forget that. I'd say you can't even get most of it done.

Go ahead and pound the sand Charlton Heston–style if you must, but once you're done mourning the myth of doing it all, let's get practical for a minute.

You only have two options right now.

1. Attempt more than is humanly possible and fail.
2. Choose what to bomb and succeed at a goal that matters.

Perfectionism tells you to take option one. In this chapter, you're going to learn how to take option two.

It's going to be uncomfortable at first. The neighbor who smokes in his driveway because his wife won't let him do it inside is going to shake his head in embarrassment at your lawn.

Unless you have a laundress, a real word that sounds like a princess of laundry, your clean-clothes chair is going to turn into a Fraggle Rock mountain of darks and whites while you work on your goal. Your kids will pick items off it like street children stealing socks from a fair.

That's OK. In moments like this, you do get to make a choice.

You can choose shame or strategy.

Say No to Shame

More than likely, you've spent most of your life choosing to do more than is possible and beating yourself up for not being able to keep up.

"I should be able to handle all of this. Yes, I've added a new goal to my life that I care about. Yes, I'm trying to put a new daily action into an already crowded calendar, but I should be able to handle it all. Yes, I moved to Atlanta to take care of my ill father-in-law, but I should be able to carry on like nothing has changed."

Our attempts to do too much feel noble and honorable. Look at us, tirelessly working toward burnout, reducing the quality of everything because we insisted we can do everything. We can share that approach with honor on Instagram. That's the grind. That's the hustle.

We often do this because we've rolled forward some bad habit we learned in high school. You could pull off an all-nighter when the final product was a ten-page essay on the effects of trade restrictions during the Civil War. It's a little harder to cram for something like your quarterly sales numbers or your weight. Eating a week's worth of kale in a single night because you're trying to get back on track with a diet is a bad plan.

At some point this catches up with you. You miss a flight and the whole fragile system falls apart. A soccer practice runs late and the plan collapses. One meeting takes too long and that dominoes into the rest of your day. A rotund family of groundhogs moves into your yard because the height of the grass provides tactical ground cover from neighboring red-tailed hawks.

Something fails, and in that moment we feel shame.

We don't pull grace out of our pocket and cut ourselves slack. No, on the contrary, most people quit right there. Not just the extra thing that proved to be too much—we give up on the whole goal.

That's the truly terrible part of trying too much. You don't just drop the bonus item and carry on with your goal. You drop every ball you're juggling when one gets out of sync, like our would-be Ironman participant from the last chapter.

When you can't do it all, you feel ashamed and give up.

Or you pick a strategy and decide in advance what things you're going to bomb.

When you choose in advance what those things will be, you remove the sting of shame. The surprise effect of shame pointing out something you're bad at is removed. Instead of reacting in shock at some ball you've dropped, you get to say, "Oh, that ball I put down on purpose before the game even started? Thanks for noticing!"

That's why Shonda Rhimes, the creator of popular shows like *Grey's Anatomy* and *Scandal,* doesn't worry about what she can't get done. When *Fast Company* asked her what she lets slide, she said, "Right now, I don't feel guilty that I'm not working out. I'll feel guilty about it at another time." When she's in the middle of running a show, actual running falls by the wayside temporarily.

Shonda said no to shame, and she could do that because she had a strategy. She had decided what she could bomb, and perfectionism couldn't torment her about missing the gym anymore.

It's OK to Be Bad at Breaking Bad

Most books like this stress your ability to get more done, not your need to identify things you can't possibly get done. But adding things to your already full life doesn't make you feel better, it just makes you feel more stressed. If you're going to avoid the shame trap, you need to decide ahead of time which activities in your life you can be bad at.

In his book *Two Awesome Hours,* Josh Davis calls this strategic incompetence. Strategic incompetence is the act of deciding ahead of time that you don't care about your yard. It's admitting you don't have time to do everything and something will deliberately go by the wayside during this season of your life.

As I started to work on my goals more aggressively, here are four things I chose to bomb:

1. Keeping up with TV conversations

    I have not watched *Breaking Bad, Stranger Things,* or *The Walking Dead.* There were sixty-two episodes of *Breaking Bad,* representing 42 minutes of content each. That's a total of 2,604 minutes, or 43 hours. That's ninety-six different 30-minute sessions you could have hustled on a goal. My friend told me he watches the entire previous season of a show before a new season starts. Every new twenty-show season really represents forty episodes to watch. I'm not against TV, and love the show *This Is Us* because I like weeping, but I can't keep up with it and with my goals. So at dinner parties when people rattle off details about popular shows I look like a huge dork and will instead make comments about *Seinfeld*. Is that wrong? Should I not do that? I tell you, I gotta plead ignorance on this thing. I'm OK with that. I've decided to stink at TV.

2. Snapchat

Perhaps by the time this book comes out I'll be amazing at Snapchat, and will be able to deftly apply puppy ears to photos of me eating lunch, but I doubt it. I have friends who keep trying to get me on it, but when I ask why, their only answer is, "Because everybody is doing it." That's the same logic that got fifty million Nickelback albums sold. People who post twenty times a day are kidding themselves when they pretend they can do long-form thought while also being interrupted constantly to let people know they're thinking. Social media isn't free; it always costs you something. I've decided to bomb Snapchat.

3. E-mail

I semiretired from e-mail a year ago. I realized that the main reason I checked it incessantly was because I'm impulsive and it made me feel important. I imagined a lot of emergencies in my in-box, but there weren't many. Now I check it a few times a week and have my assistant respond to many. Would people like it more if I responded instantly and made e-mail a constant IV drip? Maybe, but to be better at running my business and writing books, I've decided to suck at e-mail.

4. The satisfaction of cutting my own lawn

We started with my lawn; let's end there. A lot of people get deep satisfaction from mowing their grass. If you've got the kind of job where you push pixels all day, it's nice to see your effort actually add up in a physical way. Not me. As soon as I could afford twice-a-month yard service, I bailed on ever doing anything in my yard other than break dancing. (What? You use your garage for dancing instead? Fine.) I'd rather do something else with the four hours each weekend. I've decided to stink at taking care of my yard.

Strategic incompetence for me meant making peace with those four things. Will they change over time? Maybe. I might be all about Snapchat in the future. For now, though, in order for me to go all in on things that matter, I had to choose to suck at a few that don't.

In some cases, choosing to ignore something will force you to come up with a system. Most people, including me, can't fully retire from e-mail. It matters too much and represents one of the most common ways people communicate.

In order to ignore it I had to come up with a strategy. I studied the e-mails I get every day and soon realized that only 10 percent needed a personal response from me. I found that in a given week I got only a handful of e-mails that required a response within twenty-four to forty-eight hours. I had to recognize that I didn't have the personal strength to ignore the e-mail icon on my phone. My thumb goes there naturally and opens it up without me even thinking about it. I had to hide the app icon on the third page of my phone, deep inside a folder.

The thing you choose to bomb or miss out on doesn't have to be massive or permanent. When I was writing my first book, my wife pointed out that the only free time I had was on Monday. There was a two-hour window between work and a nighttime meeting I had weekly. She said, "I'll put the kids down, you write for those two hours." I didn't see my kids on Monday for twelve weeks as I worked on the book. As a dad, that wasn't easy, but I knew it was temporary and I knew it would result in a finished book.

Am I telling you to ignore your family? Yes, that's exactly what I am suggesting, because I am a monster. No, I'm just offering up a real-life example of what it takes to finish things and an explanation of why I spent two hours every Monday writing a book inside a Burger King.

What should you choose to bomb? Ultimately, it depends on what you're trying to accomplish but there is a quick way to pick a few things. Think about it like traffic lights. Some activities are green lights, they push you forward and make it easier to hit your goal. Making a week's worth of lunches might take time but it will help you reach your health goal. Other activities are red lights. They stop you from making progress and delay you. Going out late

CHOOSE WHAT TO BOMB

at night with friends might be fun, but it will tempt you to make terrible taco decisions. That's a red light activity that slows your plan to lose weight. Spend a few minutes thinking through your day and label a couple of items you're giving time to. This task is easier than you think. Putting down bark mulch in the beds in our front yard might make our house look better, but if my goal is to finish my taxes, there's no doubt what color light that is. I promise you'll be surprised how obvious some of your lights are, too.

If you can't think of something to bomb, I'll give you a head start: social media.

I know you're concerned that if you don't update your Instagram account people will notice, but I promise they won't. I once took ten days off Twitter and zero of the 290,000 people who follow me noticed.

That's why people will often deactivate their Facebook accounts during finals week or big projects. It's one less thing to worry about during a busy season. It's not forever, and in the long run the work you get done matters more.

If taking a break from social media sounds intimidating, remember, you've already done this for an entire year. It was called 1997.

Just Say No

It's one thing to stop watching TV. It's another thing to say no to spending time with friends. "I can't hang out on Friday," "No, I can't come to your event," and "I can't do you that favor" are not words we perfectionists like to say. We want to be everyone's best friend, to have every person in the world think we are wonderful, and we think that means spending as much time with every friend as he or she would like.

When you think about it, that's ridiculous.

I know that in the fall, when speaking season kicks in, I don't really get to see friends on the weekends. I travel Monday and Tuesday and then Thursday and Friday. That means the weekends belong to my family. I might be able to grab a lunch with a buddy on a Wednesday, but I can't run off to a concert with them on Saturday. For seven weeks during the fall, I bomb my friendships, to a degree.

After seven years of teaching a group of women in our small town of Franklin, Tennessee, my wife had to pause and become a student instead. She knew the fall was going to be busy and stepped down from the far more demanding role of instructor. For you, training for a race early in the morning might mean fewer nights out with friends. Starting your photography business might mean more weekends spent photographing weddings instead of spending time with friends.

There are a variety of moments that might dictate that you be more deliberate with your relationships, but they all require one thing. The easiest way to deal with people in these situations is to say the most powerful word in the English language: No.

If you're a people pleaser, I just made you want to throw up a little bit. You should never tell people no. Your answer should always be yes. No is a period. Yes is an ellipsis. It leads to new opportunities and new friends. Feel the wind on your face!

I agree, and in this book I will encourage you to share your finish with a close friend or two, but if you're really going to finish something, you will probably have to put a few other relationships on pause.

Just say no. No long explanation. No apology. No justification. No.

And remember, if someone gets mad at you for saying no, they just confirmed you were supposed to say that in the first place.

If You Can't Stop, Simplify

If a straight no makes you feel uncomfortable, or if stopping an activity is not possible, simplify instead.

One of the big-time sucks for Lisa Scheffler, a busy mom who is passionate about goal setting, is home activities. Cooking meals and doing the laundry for her family takes up a lot of time, but those are things she can't cut. She can't get focused on a goal and say, "Hey, kids, we're not going to be eating dinner this week. Good luck foraging for sustenance. Don't forget, most hipsters have pretty good gardens full of superfoods."

Instead she makes "simple meals that don't take a lot of time." And "laundry gets clean but not folded and put away, so we're a wrinkled family for a few days right before a deadline."

I love that idea. I can just see her kids all wrinkled at school and a teacher saying, "What's your mom working on this week?" And the kids know it's a big week when they see hot dogs on the table, or better yet, pizza rolls.

Fortunately, the world is more than happy to help you simplify. Staying with the food example because most of us have to eat, grocery stores now allow you to order online and pick up at the store. My wife buys 75 percent of the same things every trip. During a stressful season, she could place an order from the comfort of home, pull up, and have them place the groceries right into our trunk without even getting out of the car.

Life is too complicated for us to just say no to everything. That's fine. It's not realistic to think you can drop everything.

For situations where no isn't an option, write a "simplify list" and identify the wrinkled-shirt moments you'll be all right with in your life.

You have some meals that could be simple.

You have some things that can wait.

The Fun Starts Now

Once you get beyond the initial guilt of not being able to get everything done, choosing what to bomb becomes sort of fun. The stress of perfectionism gives way to laughter as you list the myriad things you'll no longer accept shame about.

I remember how happy my wife, Jenny, was when she quit my company. In the first two years of running my own business, Jenny had quietly slid into the role of assistant and travel agent.

If that sounds to you like the recipe for a marital disaster, you're correct.

Finally, after the thousandth work-related argument, she said, "Suck it up and pay for an assistant. I can't be a good wife and a good employee." She chose to bomb employment so she could enjoy marriage. Hiring an assistant was also a lot cheaper than marriage counseling.

That was a fun decision for Jenny to make and the ones you make will feel fun, too. But not as much as what we're going to do in the next chapter. Not even close.

Actions:

1. Make a list of three things you could bomb during your goal. Use the red light, green light approach.
2. For time drains you can't bomb, figure out a way you could simplify them.
3. Write down, in a secret place no one will see, three relationships you might need to pause in order to finish your goal.

CHAPTER 4

Make It Fun if You Want It Done

Have fun.

That's it. Two words, one clear direction. Make sure your goal is fun. Make sure you enjoy it. Make sure there's laughing and smiling involved with that thing you're going to do.

Why do I even have to write this chapter?

Why in the world would anyone ever pick a goal they didn't enjoy? Why would someone pick something boring or painful or frustrating as their New Year's resolution?

It's because perfectionism is sneaky. Perfectionism believes that the harder something is, the more miserable something is, the better it is.

The fourth lie it tells you is: Fun doesn't count.

You see this lie manifest very clearly in the two most popular forms of goals: business and health.

People want to start their own business, get their finances in order, or find their job more satisfying. They also want to eat better, get in shape, and feel good about their bodies.

So they decide to come up with a goal, and it usually goes like this:

"I want to get in shape, therefore I should run."

They start jogging, pounding the pavement before work or galloping on treadmills after. They do well for a week or two, but eventually, like the 92 percent of people who start goals, they quit.

Why?

Because they failed to ask a very simple question:

"Do I enjoy running?"

Fun is a mortal enemy of perfectionism. What's the point of joy? What's the value of fun? There's no measurable ROI on it, and it doesn't seem helpful. As a result, we never ask ourselves, "Is this fun?"

We never ask that question, assuming that if we don't like doing something it's our fault. Even as we hate the exercise each morning, we tie on our shoes, grimacing the whole time.

Perfectionism and fun are like oil and water. They don't mix. Perfectionism thinks fun is a waste of time and holds no value. Unfortunately, most of us tend to feel the same way.

Fun Counts

The reason we pursue goals we don't like is twofold:

1. We think goals have to be miserable.
2. We believe perfectionism when it tells us that fun goals don't count.

Ask people what pops into their mind when they hear the word "goal."

They will say, "Discipline, pain, striving, grind, frustration," and other words that sound horrible. We think that for a goal to be right and true, it must also be difficult. It must break us in the process or it's not a good-enough goal. The only way we'll know we've made progress is by the amount of blood, sweat, and tears we shed.

Look at the most popular form of goal setting, SMART goals. Developed decades ago, this word lays out what the creators believe each goal should be:

Specific
Measurable
Achievable
Relevant
Time-Bound

Those might be helpful attributes of a goal, but they sure are boring. Those are all words you could use to describe cauliflower. None of those words are even distant synonym cousins of the word "fun." No one has ever said, "You know what was fun about my beach vacation? It was time-bound. I knew exactly when it was going to end."

Conversely, if we have fun, the goal doesn't really count. A dance class isn't real exercise. Walking with a friend is too enjoyable to be valuable. Frisbee is for hippies. Those things aren't hard enough.

With this approach to life, you can even find a way to suck the joy out of Ping-Pong.

My goal last year was to become an amazing table tennis player. I didn't own a table, so that was my initial challenge. The second was that I didn't own a paddle. I bought one with carbon technology and a 7-ply extra light blade on Amazon because I was pretty sure I'd need that in the tournaments I was going to win. The last thing I wanted to do was show up at the club/court/dojo? with inferior equipment. I wasted far too much of my life playing with a noncarbon paddle and wasn't going to make that mistake again. I bought a carry case, too, because I'm not a chump.

What did I do next? Did I go play at the rec center with my friend Grant? Did I ask if any neighbors had a table I could play on? No, both of those options would have been far too fun and enjoyable.

Instead, I decided that the best way to learn was to find a coach. This is going to surprise you, but it's not easy to hire a table tennis coach in Nashville, Tennessee. I suppose in New York City there are coaches on every corner, but we're rich in songwriters and poor in paddlesmiths. (My term.)

I went to the Team USA Web site—you probably have it bookmarked—and discovered there are only two certified coaches in my entire state. I sent them e-mails and then waited.

Steve Chan responded. He said he was a 2,000-level player, a term I pretended to understand, and that he would evaluate me. We could play at the local rec center, except there was a power struggle going on in the Middle Tennessee table tennis community. The director of the rec center didn't approve of Chan's approach to coaching, which I assumed involved logs on your back while running through snow. Table tennis had way more politics than I initially anticipated.

I asked Steve if there was another table we could play on. He worked at an inner-city college in a transitional part of Nashville, a term that means the hipsters have not brought goat cheese ice-cream dispensaries there yet, and he said they had a table in the student union.

On a cold Saturday in February I showed up on the college campus at 4:30 to meet my table tennis coach. I confess that my hope was that he'd be exactly like Mr. Miyagi from *The Karate Kid* and that although I might learn about table tennis, ultimately I'd learn about life. I was not to be disappointed.

Steve is in his midsixties and is from mainland China. I started calling China "mainland China," because that's what Steve says, so right away I was getting an education.

Unfortunately, the student union was locked, but Steve assured me it would open momentarily. We stood there in the lobby, me with my barely used carbon-handle paddle with optional carry case because I'm not a punk and he with his sweater vest and rolling suitcase full of what I could only imagine was table tennis wizardry.

For the first twenty minutes, we made small talk while we waited for the union to open. He told me my paddle was OK, but great players order theirs in three separate pieces and assemble them. I couldn't wait to throw my junk paddle away and forge my own in my garage, like a suburban sword.

After forty minutes of showing me how to hold the paddle— you'd be surprised how many mistakes you can make with only four fingers and a thumb—we came to an uncomfortable aware- ness that the student union was never going to open. Steve then transitioned into showing me how to hit a forehand, against a mural of a jungle cat in the lobby of the building. If right now you have a mental picture of me in the lobby of a college I don't at- tend hitting a ball against an airbrushed painting of a lion on a Saturday night, you're pretty good at visualization.

"You're standing too tall and stiff, like a giraffe. You need to have an empty belly and bend like a crouching tiger. Like a tiger about to strike, loosen your muscles and get low," Steve would say. Every *Karate Kid* dream I had in my head was coming true all at once.

After thirty minutes of my losing to that wall, Steve decided I should play him. One of the keys to table tennis is the table. It's 50 percent of the name. I was unsure how Steve planned to ac- complish that feat, but again, who knows what he had in that carry-on suitcase.

Instead, he walked to the opposite edge of the circular lobby. From twenty feet away he bounced the ball softly and then hit it to me. Having never played collegiate tableless tennis, I missed the first shot.

I was also having a little trouble with the sheer quantity of the awkwardness. Occasionally, college students would walk by to check if the student union was open. If you're picturing a bewildered nineteen-year-old college student staring at a forty-one-year-old man playing table tennis against an elderly sensei in a sweater vest in the lobby without a table, you're still doing great. That is exactly what was happening.

In total, we played for two hours.

In the lobby.

Without a table.

For the rest of the lessons, we met at a local club. For hours at a time he would hit a hundred balls at me, slowly teaching me forehand, backhand, and the push.

I wasn't ready for a tournament yet. Steve didn't believe I was ready to actually play a game, something we never did once during our entire training relationship, which only lasted four lessons. If that feels brief, I promise it's not. I'm a starter, not a finisher, so doing something four times in a row is actually a personal record.

I didn't quit because I hated table tennis. I quit because I wasn't having fun. Instead of just buying a table and playing with friends, I was paying twenty dollars an hour to run drills with an elderly stranger who would yell "Kill, kill, kill" at me, indicating that if this were a game he would have killed my pathetic return shot.

Regardless of the type of goal, my belief that goals must be difficult and joyless will wreck me at every turn.

Many of us do this. We crave challenges that make us miserable, which is why adventure races are so popular right now.

When the Tough Mudder race initially started, one of the obstacles you had to navigate was a field of live electrical wires. You spend your entire life trying to prevent your skin from ever touching a live wire, but on Tough Mudder day, you pay for that experience.

When I was eight, I tried to press the coin return button on a Skee-Ball machine at Chuck E. Cheese's. The button was missing and instead of getting my token back, my finger touched an open wire. It felt like my entire hand was getting chewed up by a meat grinder made of fire and wasps.

That's the sensation you pay for at Tough Mudder.

Mind you, this is after you've jumped into a dumpster full of ice, so that every muscle in your body rejects the instructions from your brain and collapses you on the ground involuntarily. Only then do you get to crawl through a muddy pit, your back grazing against hundreds of wires. Participant Dino Evangelista described the experience as "feeling like a giant had punched me between the shoulders into the ground as hard as he could." The T-shirt you get better be amazing.

Those aren't goals, those are forms of torture. That's why my counselor asked me to quit reading self-help books for a while. I was OD'ing on tired tomes that only made me feel like a failure. I'd buy each new book, hoping secretly that it would be harder to follow through on than the last one, with deeper mud and more hot wires.

I thought that progress had to feel that way. I thought fun didn't count.

That's a lie. Fun not only counts, but it's necessary if you want to beat perfectionism and get to the finish.

Fun goals win.

The crazy thing is that the aggressively nonfun approach doesn't work. It might make you look good on Instagram as you impress your friends with your miserable grind, but scientifically speaking, joyless goals fail.

When you study goal setting you look at a variety of statistical factors, but the two most interesting are: (1) satisfaction, and (2) performance success. One speaks to how you felt about the process and the second focuses on what you actually got done.

A great finishing principle will dramatically increase both. It doesn't do either of us any good if I teach you something that increases your satisfaction but decreases your performance success. You'll be smiling all the way to last place. And if your performance success soars while your satisfaction plummets, you'll be a miserable winner.

This is why some of the most outwardly successful people you know are some of the saddest. They crushed the second metric but forgot the first mattered, too. This was why I was getting better at table tennis but wasn't really having fun. To have a great principle, both satisfaction and performance success must be present. Fun is one of those approaches that checks both boxes.

If the thousands of participants in the 30 Days of Hustle program are any indication, choosing a goal you believe will be enjoyable increases your likelihood of satisfaction by 31 percent. This might be the most obvious scientific conclusion ever made. Of course your satisfaction level will go up when you do something you enjoy. This just in: Eating ice cream is fun!

But that's not where the research ends. The second benefit to picking something you enjoy is that it increases performance success by 46 percent. You perform better when you pick something you think is fun.

Study after study has confirmed this. The common myth about high-level performance is that it must be grueling, painful, and difficult. But the scientists researching elite swimmers found to their surprise that even at the 5:30 A.M. practices, the swimmers "were lively, laughing, talking, enjoying themselves." They continued, "It is incorrect to believe that top athletes suffer great sacrifices to achieve their goals. Often, they don't see what they do as sacrificial at all. They like it."

Crawl in the mud all you want, open-mouth kiss electrical wires. Fill your pants with moray eels. I don't care. The best way to accomplish something is just the opposite of all that. Fun isn't optional. It's necessary if you're going to kill perfectionism and make it through to done.

Kale Isn't Fun

What if the goal you want to accomplish isn't naturally fun?

Losing weight isn't inherently fun.

It's not.

Feeling like you're going to throw up because you're on a treadmill isn't fun.

Stumbling through exercises you don't really know yet isn't fun.

Getting up early isn't fun.

Syrupy positive books that tell you otherwise are dumb.

But keep in mind that the shortcut isn't "find something fun"; the shortcut is "make it fun if you want it done." There's action involved in that. You have to do the work of making it fun. How?

Ask this question: "How could this goal be more fun?"

Crazy, right? I know. I'm a visionary.

Most of us don't add fun to our goals. Have you ever asked that question about any goal you've ever undertaken? At work, did a boss lay out the strategy for the third quarter and then say, "Bear in mind, this has to be fun!" If you've ever made a New Year's resolution, did you make sure it was fun? Was that a prerequisite? Was that something you planned for?

Fun isn't part of the language we use when it comes to hard work, hustle, or discipline. But this is another example of going on offense against perfectionism. If we can short-circuit its wires by saying fun is actually important, we are more likely to finish the task.

Jeremy Cowart found a way to make his goal fun when he started Help-Portrait. Cowart, a widely successful photographer, wanted to "give back." That's a pretty popular goal and most people don't think it can be fun. They instantly think, "I have to build a house for someone, paint a rec center, or serve soup downtown." We never start our volunteer work by saying, "What's something I really enjoy doing that I could use to serve someone?" And more often than not, we give up on giving back.

Cowart made fun a priority. After a decade shooting people like Taylor Swift and Garth Brooks, he knew the power of a well-taken photo. He knew the confidence and joy that comes from seeing yourself all made up for a portrait. He also knew that if he loved the project enough, he would keep going. He started offering free portraits at a special event held every year at hundreds of locations around the world. People get their makeup done for free, sit for a six-figure photographer, and many times walk away with the only portrait they've ever had taken.

To date, Help-Portrait has taken more than half a million photos.

You know what Jeremy doesn't do? He doesn't swing a hammer or a paint roller. Why? He's not good at it, but more than that, it's not fun to him. And he knows that the more joy he feels, the longer he'll work at something that helps other people.

It's easy to find the fun in his story. What if you don't know how to make something fun? Where do you begin? There are two places.

Fun Comes in Two Very Different Flavors.
Choose Wisely.

Ben Rains is a financial adviser, but math rarely persuades his clients to make the best decisions. He can lay out the numbers. He can crunch the data perfectly. He can flow chart and graph until his printer runs out of ink, but until he's answered one question about his clients, none of that matters.

What do they really think is fun?

Everyone he sits down with to talk finances brings something unique to the table. They are buffeted by unseen waves, like how their parents handled money growing up, the health of their romantic relationships, what they care about the most, and a million other factors, but in a decade of helping people he's found that client motivations fall into two rough categories:

1. Reward motivation
2. Fear motivation

For some people, once the reward is detailed and clear, some sort of motivational engine is fired up. Once the path to retirement or paying for college is laid out, they run down it with vigor.

People who are motivated by a reward have what psychologists call an approach motivation. They are wired to approach the reward that accomplishing a certain goal will generate. The positive outcome is what drives them. That's their version of fun. Seeing their first sale come in on an online store is the vision they hold closest when building a new business. Putting on a pair of jeans that haven't fit in years and going shopping for new clothes with a new figure is what matters most. Having the freedom to buy something without checking a bank account nervously is the feeling that bubbles to the top. They are motivated by the prize associated with achieving the goal.

For others, a reward doesn't move the needle at all. The pretty picture of the future is too far off, too boring, or too safe. Dreaming about retirement when you're thirty is like trying to tell fifteen-year-olds they'll get a great job someday if they focus on their high school studies.

They are not motivated by what could be if they acted; they are driven by what won't be if they don't. The fear that their kids won't be able to go to college jolts them awake. A future where there is no Florida and they must work until the day they die shocks them into action. The fear of the future forces them to change the present.

This is called avoidance motivation. People motivated this way are not trying to achieve a desired outcome, they are trying to prevent an undesired outcome. Fear in those cases isn't a fire-breathing dragon, it's a cold bucket of water. It's an alarm clock that wakes you up, giving you a kick in the pants to get moving. I feel that type of fear every time I get ready to speak at an event. I practice harder for the speech knowing that I don't want to experience the feeling of bombing.

We might not naturally associate the word "fear" with fun, but if you're wired for avoidance motivation you know exactly what I'm talking about. There's a certain rush to dodging a bullet or just beating a deadline at the last second. Disaster averted can be a very motivating feeling.

There are times when jokes don't work. There are times when the audience doesn't like me. But it's not because I was unprepared. My worst fear is that I'm booked for an hour-long speech and finish all my material in twenty minutes. I'm not that scared when I stand on stage anymore, but the thought of being marooned up there with the hot lights, staring eyes, and expectant faces without anything to say haunts me. In that way, I'm not a people pleaser, I'm a people not-displeaser. It's not a great title yet. I'm still workshopping it.

I don't particularly care about the applause. I like the laughter, I enjoy that, but what motivates me more is the silence. I work hard to be funny or interesting or helpful so that I don't displease people. I'm not motivated by approaching cheering, I'm motivated by avoiding jeering.

My favorite part of an entire event is getting in my car in the parking lot at the airport. That's when I know I did it. I finished. I didn't bomb. I was prepared and it's done.

If you're motivated by fear, don't fight it as an adversary. Use it.

Cus D'Amato, Floyd Patterson and Mike Tyson's trainer during the healthy years, knew the importance of fear. "You must understand fear so you can manipulate it. Fear is like fire.

You can make it work for you: it can warm you in the winter, cook your food when you're hungry, give you light when you are in the dark, and produce energy. Fear is a friend of exceptional people."

Understanding what kind of fun moves you, whether it's moving toward a rosy future or avoiding a grim eventuality, is important data for you to have.

So which is it?

Parents with two kids will understand this exercise because what motivates one kid bores another. Losing access to a video game will inspire your daughter to clean her room. Losing access to that same game will make your other daughter yawn. She's community-motivated anyway and is more than happy to give up a solitary activity like that.

In the past, have you been driven by fear or by reward? Are you inspired by the thought of sailing back into the harbor successfully or preventing a shipwreck deep at sea? As author Jonathan Fields says, is your goal to push a failure away from yourself or pull a victory toward yourself?

Failing to recognize what is "fun" or motivating is a big part of why goals often fail. It's like having the right car, but the wrong key. I experienced this at the gym once. In the parking lot, a woman asked me for help with her husband's car. Nothing she tried with the remote would work. The doors stayed locked, the key didn't fit, and even the trunk wouldn't open. After several laps around the SUV, I looked closer at the key chain and realized it had a big VW on it. That wasn't a problem, except her car was a Ford. I then turned my head and saw a white VW Jetta across the parking lot with the trunk wide open. She had accidently taken someone else's keys from the gym lockers.

When you use the wrong form of motivation, you'll never get the car to move. A doctor tells you that if you don't lose weight, you'll increase your chances of serious health issues. That's a fear motivation, but if you're motivated by reward, all the warnings in the world will roll right off your back. A better approach might be to find a reward, like being healthy enough to finally hike Cinque Terre in Italy, a coastal trail that cascades through five brightly colored cities between Genoa and Pisa.

When your boss assigns you a project no one wants with a team no one likes, the temptation is to wait for motivation to show up. You'll never finish anything, though, if you wait to be inspired. Instead, pick which form of motivation you need the most and then add it to as many parts of the project as possible.

Motivated by the fear of a deadline? Create a dozen small deadlines in the project. Motivated by the reward you get when your efforts are recognized by others? Do a weekly update that you send to all the key stakeholders, describing the progress of the project. Motivated by rewards? Add some personal prizes along the way. When author Sammy Rhodes had a huge project due he would reward himself with a movie if he completed his work. The promise of a Friday afternoon film made the work on Thursday all the easier.

As you choose between fear and a reward, please know that perfectionism will tell you that you don't need either. Real winners don't need motivation. They just do their job. They don't need rewards or punishments, no carrots or sticks. They just put their nose to the grindstone. A reward is cheating. You're better than that. The hard work is its own reward.

The minute you hear anything like that, you'll know you're on the right path. Perfectionism only gets loud when people get moving.

Real People Using Real Fun in Real Ways

My friend posted on Instagram that she was enjoying a guilty pleasure on a flight. What was she imbibing? Seltzer water.

That's right, you freaking heathen, her guilty pleasure is seltzer water—not even tonic. She's drinking straight seltzer water. How bad do you feel about your life choices right now? My guilty pleasures usually involve ignoring a serving-size suggestion. Have you ever eaten a whole package of something before you noticed it said "share size" or "party pack"? That party was not supposed to be just for you.

You know what, though, that's awesome that my friend rewards herself with seltzer water. Why? Because fun is supposed to be personal and often that means it's weird.

That's why I lit a balsam and cedar candle when I sat down to write this chapter. It's not even December, the official month of balsam and cedar. That's like listening to Mariah Carey's

Christmas album in June, but I don't even care. I live by my own rules.

I love the smell of balsam. I probably picked it up when I bought an ax I never really used. The woods change a man, I suppose. Regardless of the origin of my love, I'm a huge fan of that scent. It smells like Christmas and reindeer and happiness. So during the writing of this book, I bought a sixty-hour candle at Yankee Candle. I committed to lighting it only when I was writing this book.

Doing this was also a reminder that most people are not either-or when it comes to reward and fear motivation. Fear motivates me to prepare my speeches but a reward encourages me to work hard at my writing.

This was fun for me on two levels. The first is the smell, which is magical, like a unicorn's breath. The second is watching the progress of the wax. I really wanted to get to the bottom of the candle. I envisioned putting the empty jar up on my shelf when it was finished. I'd stare up at it in victory, knowing that I single-handedly slayed that candle.

Is that weird? It is. It definitely is.

But that's not any weirder than going to the gym five days in a row at 5 A.M. so you can earn a free T-shirt. That's what scores of people at my gym did during Hell Week, a weeklong torture fest that ended with a free T-shirt. Along the way, you got an orange star next to your name on a big board for every day you completed.

The sticker might feel a bit like kindergarten, but I promise you I saw grown adults giddy with each one they earned.

Weird works, and perfectionism absolutely hates it. Of course it would. If it's opposed to fun, can you imagine how much disregard it has for weirdness? Perfectionism is about conformity, it's about twisting and molding your performance to some imaginary standard that's impossible to hit. There's no room for weird when it comes to perfectionism.

Sometimes, instead of picking between a reward or a loss, you can knock out two birds with one stone. When Emily Bortz did a weight-loss challenge with her sister, the loser had to pay for the winner's massage. In addition to being motivated by the reward of the massage, you could be motivated by the fear of paying for one you weren't receiving.

OK, we've now exhausted our quota of weight-loss examples, but what about something boring like housework? Here's how Stephen Nazarian, one of my readers, approaches it.

"I have a never-ending 'honey-do' list around the house. Many of the items only take fifteen to twenty minutes (like changing some switch plates or hanging a frame). So, whenever I'm shot from the day and just want to relax in the Jacuzzi tub, I force myself to start a short task on the list and when I'm almost done I go turn on the water for the tub and let it fill while I finish. I've done this so much that now I can't relax in the Jacuzzi without doing something productive first. Pavlov would be proud."

Is there anything weirder than using a Jacuzzi to condition yourself to be more productive? I submit *no*. That's why I love Stephen.

The size of the reward can vary as well as the type. I decided one year that every time I had to go on a business trip, I was going to reward myself by upgrading the rental car.

In Seattle, I asked the Enterprise guy how much it would cost to upgrade my car. He looked at his tablet and said, "I can get you from the sewing machine you currently have rented and into an Infiniti for twenty dollars a day." In Charlotte, a brand-new Volvo cost fifteen dollars. In Dallas, a Cadillac was twenty dollars.

That might not seem like much of a reward, but if you've ever traveled for business, little things like that make all the difference. I was going to spend three hours in the car in Seattle. Driving a fast, fun model made the trip infinitely better and cost me twenty dollars.

That was a small reward. When I completed the first draft of this book, I bought ski boots. I had the money prior to finishing the book, and I could have purchased them before I completed the goal, but that would have ruined the reward.

What about the flip side, if you're motivated by fear? It's often hard to think of a punishment version if you don't hit the goal, but don't be afraid to get creative. The cocreator of the show *Billions* and cowriter of the movie *Rounders,* Brian Koppelman, once had a movie script he just couldn't get financed. People in the business told him it would be impossible because of the dark subject matter. The financiers would never go along with his plan and it was a hopeless situation. Finally, after a few frustrating months, he went to Nike.com and designed an incredibly ugly pair of sneakers. Written across them in bright pink was the name of the movie he was working on. He had to wear the hideous shoes until he finished. That day he dedicated himself to taking at least one concrete action each day.

Weird? Sure. But ask Michael Douglas if he liked starring in the movie *Solitary Man,* which Brian did get financed.

Radio host David Hooper once hired a career coach who had an interesting approach to the fear versus reward spectrum. He made Hooper write out a check that the coach would send to the political party Hooper hated the most if he didn't hit his goals. The coach had the check, so the process was automatic. If David didn't work on his goal, the candidate he can't stand would get a little support. Worst of all, now he'd be on the party's mailing list, a nightmarish database you will never escape from, my friend.

What's your reward going to be? Or if you're more motivated by fear, what's the threat?

Remember, perfectionism will tell you that fun doesn't count. Even worse, it will tell you that using rewards or fears as a form of motivation to reach your goal is a crutch. You're the only one with stupid, fun, weird systems.

Only you're not.

Right now, I'm probably practicing a speech somewhere so I don't bomb. I'm lighting a candle that smells like the forest so I can keep writing. A stay-at-home mom is going shopping because she lost the amount of weight that triggered a reward.

The more fun you add to your goal, be it in the form of fear or reward, the more likely you'll actually finish.

How to Read a Hundred Books a Year

In January and February of 2017, I read eighteen books. That was undoubtedly the most I've ever read in such a short time frame. I probably read fewer books than that in all of 2016.

How did I do it? How did the guy who started this book by confessing he'd only finished 10 percent of the books he owns turn it around? I used fun.

First of all, I expanded my definition of "what counts." I decided audiobooks counted. Not just audiobooks, but audiobooks at 1.5x speed. Some authors read their books soooooo slowly. I also didn't give myself a page limit for what I defined as a book. If I wanted to read a 120-page short idea from a business author, that counted. I read some 700-page books during the year, but not every one I picked up had to be as thick as a phone book. I also decided to read graphic novels. As soon as I said that online, someone said, "Do comic books count?"

Against what? What invisible standard was my personal goal of reading a hundred books in a year supposed to be measured against? Who's quality level was I judging my goal based on? I made the rules and I decided to make them fun. I like audiobooks, and I like comic books, so I made sure they counted.

I also made sure to set in place fun rewards for myself. Every time I finished a book, I would post it on Instagram with a short review and the hashtag #AcuffReadsBooks. (You can check the hashtag right now; all the books are still up.) I liked the discussions each post generated and always got great recommendations for other books from people. But that's not what was fun.

What was fun was seeing them stack up. I'm a numbers guy, and watching the list get bigger, the collection of images swelling each time I finished one, was enjoyable. I'm also motivated by an audience. It didn't hurt my feelings that people said things like "Wow, you're reading a ton of books this year!" I am, complete stranger, thanks for noticing. The affirmation, even from people I didn't know, was really fun to me.

That's a little embarrassing. Perfectionism told me I shouldn't need the approval of other people to accomplish a goal. I should be able to be motivated by my own personal sense of satisfaction. I was being vain and needy. Someone smarter, someone with a healthier sense of self, wouldn't have to share what they were doing.

Maybe not. I bet that perfect person recycles really well, too, even when they eat at Whole Foods and there are nineteen different recycling bins and it takes you half an hour to throw your trash away. But that's not me.

Who am I?

I'm the guy who read more than a hundred books in 2017 because I thought a hashtag and some support from random followers was fun.

The Truth About Fun

> Working hard for something we don't care about is called stress. Working hard for something we love is called passion.
>
> —Simon Sinek

Perfectionism must hate this book right now. Let's review the three actions I've recommended:

1. Cut your goal in half.
2. Choose what you'll bomb.
3. Make it fun if you want it done.

Easiest goal-setting book ever.

Seriously, what kind of task is "Have more fun?"

I'll tell you. It's the kind of task that statistically works.

It's the kind of task that kills perfectionism.

It's the kind of task that will propel you across the finish line.

But if you really want to get there, you'll have to give up something first. It's time to let go of some hiding places and ignore your noble obstacles.

Actions:

1. On a scale of 1 to 10, how fun is the goal you might be working on?

2. Decide whether you're motivated by fear or by reward.

3. Fun is often weird. (See balsam candle.) To flesh it out a little, finish this sentence: "This is weird, but I find _____ fun."

4. Pick three small points of fun you can add to your goal.

CHAPTER 5

Leave Your Hiding Places
and Ignore Noble Obstacles

In 2004, I created a wildly successful fantasy basketball news-letter.

Right now, you're wondering if it was one of the many fantasy basketball newsletters you read during those heady days of digital NBA journalism. It might have been, friend, it might have been.

Every week, I would deep dive into the many ups and downs of managing a fantasy basketball team. (Sports guys like me call the NBA "the widow maker." Tough league.)

I'd review each team, dozens of players, and trends that the data was subtly revealing. I didn't dryly write, either; I peppered my prose with humor. You might think you were going to get just an analysis of the top rebounders in the league, but mingled in there were a chuckle and maybe even a life lesson.

Some issues were ten pages long, with thousands of words dedicated to the most obscure minutiae. It was hard work, but the readers, fans really, made it all worth it.

How many people read it each week? How many people enjoyed my hard-won basketball knowledge? Eight.

Not eight thousand. Not eight hundred. Not even eight dozen. My entire audience was eight people deep. So then why did I dedicate hours every week to the newsletter?

Because it was a lot easier than writing a book.

At the beginning of any goal, perfectionism focuses on destroying it with a full frontal attack.

It tells you that if it isn't perfect, you should quit.

It says your goal isn't big enough.

It criticizes you for even thinking about making it fun.

But if you hold on, if you refuse to allow perfectionism to denigrate your goal, it will completely change tactics. Unexpectedly, it will move from destruction to distraction.

If it can't break your wall down with a direct attack, it will lay siege to you with other opportunities.

The closer you get to finishing, the more interesting everything else in your life becomes. It's as if you've put on distraction goggles. Things you never noticed pop up and dance tantalizingly across your vision. "Wouldn't it be better to organize your bookshelf than finish that project? Have you updated your Fantasy Football team in a while? You know, there's a book somewhere that said networking is important. Maybe you should ignore this paperwork and take a quick lap around the office to rub some elbows." (You should never rub a coworker's elbows. That's creepy. Terrible phrase.)

When we dare to focus, a thousand other things beg for our attention.

Everyone has heard the phrase "paralysis by analysis." You can get stuck drawing a perfect plan and never actually get work done if you're not careful.

But more than just analysis, perfectionism offers us two distinct distractions:

1. Hiding places
2. Noble obstacles

A hiding place is an activity you focus on instead of your goal.

A noble obstacle is a virtuous-sounding reason for not working toward a finish.

Both are toxic to your ability to finish.

Hiding Places

Let's discuss hiding places first. A hiding place is the safe place you go to hide from your fear of messing up. It's the task that lets you get your perfectionism fix by making you feel successful even as you avoid your goal.

Some hiding places are easily spotted as the unproductive traps they are. If you're watching Netflix every time it's time for you to do X, that's a hiding place. You're afraid to face the fear of imperfection that comes along with every endeavor, so you're hiding from it by doing something that requires no skill. You might write a bad sentence on your blog, but no one's going to critique the way you watch TV. "I just feel like he could be doing a better job of fast-forwarding through the opening credits of each show."

Other hiding places can look like productivity, but they're deceptive. Like quicksand. Quicksand doesn't look that different from a regular beach. (If you Google Image search "quicksand," in addition to finding photos of women in bikinis, because God forbid a single Internet search not return that, you find some very boring looking photos of sand.) Quicksand looks like the tide has recently gone out on the shore. But it's actually sand that has liquefied and the weight you put on it sucks you deeper down into it.

Hiding places are tricky like that. They make you feel like you're doing well when in reality you're not getting anywhere on your most important projects.

My wife, Jenny, calls me out on hiding places all the time. One afternoon she said, "I know you're avoiding writing when your in-box is immaculate."

As I mentioned earlier, I hate e-mail. I hate my in-box. I hate everything about that form of communication. But when I have other work I need to finish, it provides the perfect hiding place for me. It's never done. There's always one more folder to empty and one more contact to stay in touch with. I can write a perfect e-mail and feel great about myself for working hard.

The best/worst part is that when you empty your in-box by

responding to people, it just guarantees that they will respond, which means your in-box is full again. It's a never-ending cycle, like the ocean tide. Plus, I can justify it by saying that I'm making money by responding to opportunities. I can feel like a good business owner by answering questions for customers. I get all the buzz of accomplishment with very little of the real work.

I'd write the best book ever if I didn't have so many e-mails! Oh, cruel world, and your constantly returning e-mails. I wish I weren't so busy.

If you're going to finish, you have to ignore these two hiding places. Here are a few simple ways to identify them:

1. Do you find yourself going there accidentally?

If you blink and find yourself working on something besides your real goal, you've probably retreated to the first kind of hiding place: the obvious time waster. You will never accidentally end up doing a difficult project. The work you're trying to avoid is not something you'll stumble upon one day unexpectedly. "I just looked up and I was sorting through all the job applications people had sent in. It was a task I'd put off for weeks, but there it was!" You'll never accidentally work out. "I meant to watch TV, but the next thing I knew, I was doing burpees!" Difficult work requires discipline. The hiding places perfectionism offers don't. You don't have to tell yourself to bite your nails if you're a nail-biter. It just happens. Especially during stress. Is there a project you keep returning to? One you can't let go of? I once spent hours trying to craft

1

a perfect postcard for The Home Depot. Finally, my boss came over and reminded me that no one was going to remember that postcard. But every executive we reported to was going to review the new catalog I was supposed to be writing. It represented a gigantic shift in our business and was really difficult to finish. I would much rather screw around with the postcard than deal with the catalog. It was a lot easier to accidentally stumble back into the postcard project than it was to work on the bigger project. What's the app you open up on your phone without even thinking? We all have one of those. You barely touch your phone and next thing you know, you're scrolling through Instagram.

2. Do you have to play Six Degrees of Kevin Bacon to justify why you're giving it time?

If you ever have to do a complicated, multistep explanation to say why what you're doing is valuable, it probably isn't. You're probably actually camping out in the kind of hiding place that masquerades as productivity. I could have argued that running a fantasy basketball league was teaching me how to build an audience with consistent content. That has the perfect appearance of being helpful, until you peel the onion a little. If you spend days and weeks building an audience that likes the funny way you write about basketball, what makes you think that same audience is going to love your comical insights about goal setting? What's that transition going to look like? "You know how you love my thoughts on Michael Jordan's vertical leap? What about a book I wrote about my inability to complete projects? See how those are related!" Only they're not. I would have to jump at least a few steps away from my real goal, of writing a book, to justify my basketball newsletter. Is what you're working on directly in line with what you want to finish, or is it disconnected by a few steps that take some creativity to explain?

3. What do your friends think?

If you really want to find a hiding place, ask a friend. It's easy to deceive yourself by thinking a task is useful, and we can't identify it as a hiding place as quickly as a friend can. Ask someone close to you if you're spending time, energy, or money on something that's not important to your goals—and don't listen to perfectionism when it tells you not to do this. Perfectionism loves isolation. It would prefer you go it alone, convincing you that relying on others is cheating. You should just be strong enough not to need anybody. That's ridiculous. Why does it tell you that? Because it's easier to beat one person than it is a team. And most of the worst decisions you've ever made were made alone. That's why.

The goal of those questions is to get a few hiding places identified.

Once you identify the hiding places, the logical thing is to take the time, energy, and money you are spending in the hiding place and spend them on the activities that help you meet your goals.

If you want to write an album, do the things it takes to write an album. I don't know what those are, but I know they all require time, energy, and probably money.

If you identify one of these hiding places, you should stop going there with your time. The hour you spent watching TV is gone forever. You might, as Bon Jovi sang, wake up with an iron-clad fist and French kiss the morning, but that hour will never come back. Also, grossest line in a love song. What does that even mean? If you saw someone on a plane wake up from a nap and French kiss the morning, you'd call a sky marshal.

Energy is a little more difficult to measure, but is just as expensive as time. Einstein did his best work when he was employed at the ever-boring patent office. Why did this help him? Because his mundane job didn't drain him creatively. He came home with full reserves. Don't spend your energy on hiding places if you can help it.

Finally, stop spending money on your hiding places. If you can't afford to go to the gym you really like because you don't have the money, expensive vacations might be a hiding place.

You have a limited amount of time, energy, and money. We all do.

If something is stealing from any of those reserves, be careful.

The flip side is that some things aren't distractions, they're commitments.

Your corporate job, for instance, might not be something you love, but it's not a hiding place, it's a commitment. Giving that time and energy is what you should do. Your kids are not distractions. This one was hard for me because when they were young my kids dropped their afternoon nap. If you don't have kids, that might not sound like a big deal, but if you do, you know exactly how painful that is. And we didn't discuss this or get to vote on it either. One day they just decided, You know what? We're done with that nap. You know those ninety minutes you treasured each Saturday afternoon? We're liberating them. They belong to us. We're captains now.

Just like that, they were gone.

This is going to happen to you. Your kid will get up at the same time every day for a solid year, right up until the morning you decide to get up early to work on something. On that morning, she will pop out of bed early and ask you an awful lot of questions about Go-Gurt. But that's OK. Your kids are commitments. So is your health. So is your spouse.

But that project that you always work on rather than move toward your dreams? Those hours spent doing X instead of what really matters? It's time to recognize that the peace hiding places give you is a false one. They don't protect you—instead, they keep you from reaching your goals. It's time to recognize hiding places for the perfectionism trap they are and to step out into the light.

Even more important, it's time to turn hiding-place activities into tools that will help you make it to the finish.

Time for a Little Judo

As anyone who has struggled with hiding places knows, one of the best ways to fall in love with a new goal is to just try to finish an old one.

You are never more creative for new ideas than when you are almost done with an old one.

"What's next" will always look more interesting than "what's now."

Please know that the minute you pick a goal and make it fun, a new goal that's really a hiding place will pop into your head. I don't mean eventually, I don't mean later, I don't mean on Day 14. I mean on Day 1. Before you've even left the harbor, perfectionism will have some other port calling your name.

Faced with this temptation, you will do the worst possible thing, which is to try to kill it.

I've got to focus, you will say to yourself.

I've got to ignore it, you will shout.

In a matter of minutes, you'll be right back to your old habit of trying harder. If you'd just try harder, you wouldn't be so distracted. Cue perfectionism.

But what if that's not a distraction but a great idea? What if that new thing that came out of seemingly nowhere is actually something you should definitely do? What if that's the best idea you've ever had and it got stirred up by all your hard work?

I don't know if it is, but I know that ignoring it is the wrong approach.

Fighting it is a waste of time and energy. Instead, embrace it. Admit that it might indeed be awesome. And then make exploring it a condition of finishing the goal you are working on.

In judo, you don't try to stop an opponent's power, you use it. You take his momentum and weight and strength. You don't push back against a charging foe, you lean backward and allow the rush to topple your opponent unexpectedly. That's what you should do when a distraction gets too loud.

For example, I want to start a podcast. I've wanted to start one for a while, but I didn't really get passionate about it until I tried to finish this book. As soon as I buckled down to writing this, you'd be surprised how attractive that podcast became. I could rattle off my future guests, list the questions I'd ask them, and discuss how I would grow the audience with the greatest of ease.

Instead of feeling shame and trying to ignore that project, I placed it directly after the finish line for this book.

I didn't say never; I said later.

Want to create a reward you really love? When new ideas or new goals get shiny, put them at the finish line. Don't try to grow callous to the shiny objects; if anything, let them gleam. Let them be brighter than the noonday sun. Just make sure they point the way to the finish line.

No podcast until the book is done.

No other diet until you've finished the one you already committed to.

No other small business idea until you've completed the original one.

Line your finish line with the dream goals you're currently using as hiding places and then watch how fast you'll run toward it.

Beware the Noble Obstacle

A noble obstacle is what perfectionism throws at you next if you deal with the hiding places. It's the Very Good Reason you cannot pursue your goal. Perfectionism will tell you, "If you're going to do it, you might as well do it right." And when we leave the idea of "right" undefined, it tends to get complicated, usually in one of two ways.

In the first kind of noble obstacle, perfectionism sneakily tells you that you cannot move toward your goal *until* you do something else: "I can't do X until Y." In the second kind, perfectionism tells you that reaching your goal could actually produce bad results or make you a bad person.

Would-be entrepreneurs often express fear that they'll become workaholics if they start a business. They're one step away from a messy divorce if they dare make a go at their goal and that's just not worth it. Better to play it safe and just think about what they could have done if they really wanted to. They're not avoiding the business, they're protecting the sanctity of the marriage. How noble.

A noble obstacle is the reason Bill is never going to clean his garage.

Bill knows he will never meet his goal. Every time he uses the small travel paths through the suburban rubble, he is well aware of the fact that he will most likely be dead before this garage is cleaned. He probably doesn't think this when he is getting a drink from the fridge because that's pretty dark, but it's true.

I don't blame him. The one time I cleaned our garage I found a foot-long Norwegian wharf rat, which was weird because we didn't live near a wharf or Norway. They're also called the "brown rat" or the "we need to sell this house" rat. It would be great if your garage rat was more *The Secret of NIMH* and less steal your car radio, but it never works out that way.

I don't know whether Bill has rats, but I know he can't announce to his wife that he will never clean his garage.

Instead, when pressured by her to clean it, he says, "Great idea! I will. Let's have a garage sale first!"

On the surface, this feels a bit like the best step toward the completion of the goal.

He didn't argue, he actually agreed to the project, enthusiastically so. Not only does he consent to it, he adds a way they can make money through the project. That's a win-win right there.

But his wife knows what he is doing.

Bill is not taking the first step toward cleaning the garage. he is employing a noble obstacle.

At the heart of it, a noble obstacle is an attempt to make your goal harder than it has to be so you don't have to finish, but can still look respectable.

Writing a fantasy basketball newsletter instead of writing a business book is a hiding place.

Deciding that you can't write your book until you've read the top one hundred business books of all time is a noble obstacle.

Bill and his wife haven't had a garage sale once in the twenty years they've been married. He's never wanted to have one. He doesn't go to them on the weekends. He never even mentioned the idea until he was pushed into a corner. At that moment he created a noble obstacle.

Think about the myriad steps a garage sale adds to the real intent of the project: an empty garage. Here are just a few of the extra tasks:

1. Pick a perfect day for the sale, checking the weather, your business travel plans, and your kids' soccer schedule.
2. Review your HOA to make sure there aren't any weird rules about garage sales.
3. Make signs advertising the sale: WHARF RAT FOR A GOOD HOME.
4. Hang the signs up.
5. Research garage sales on Pinterest so that your sale looks appealing, like a cake pop.
6. Clean the garage so that you actually know what you're selling.
7. Sort items into "sell," "throw away," and "keep."
8. Decide on prices for all the items.
9. Label the items with price tags.

10. Display the items in your driveway.
11. Go to the bank to make sure you have enough spare change for the two people on the planet who still pay with cash.
12. Set up a Square account so that you can take debit cards.
13. Hold the sale.
14. Negotiate with the weirdos who regularly shop at yard sales.
15. Sort through the items that didn't sell.
16. Replace any leftover items in the garage.

What was a one-step goal—clean garage—turned into a sixteen-step project.

Is it any wonder this noble obstacle will ensure that Bill never actually does anything with the garage? His wife would have been happy if he'd gutted the garage with a flamethrower, but in the face of such a wonderfully noble obstacle, her hands are tied.

Bill is not alone. We all have our noble obstacles. You have some, too.

"Until" Will Kill You

Some noble obstacles are personal and unique. They're tailor-made to you and would be impossible to detail in a book that millions of people will read. (Speaking that into reality.) Others are common and easily identified, such as the word "until." I've used this one in my own life many times.

"I can't do my taxes until I know what kind of business I'm really trying to build."

I told this to a friend, who laughed at me.

I was attempting to tell him that until I had a deep purpose, which I've already written about, a perfect mission for my business and really my whole life, I couldn't figure out a way to make my taxes easier. "Until" is just perfectionism wearing a Halloween costume.

Karen won't start her blog until she's checked in with a copyright lawyer first.

She is concerned that her blog will become so successful that someone will steal the content. She wrote me an e-mail and expressed her concern that this thief will steal her royalties on T-shirts, foam hats, and the graphic novel adaptation. As a fellow writer, I can't tell you how much cash I've made from the thriving foam hat industry.

That might seem like a silly worry, but how often are our worries rational?

This is such a great example of the first kind of noble obstacle, because how easy is it to find a good copyright lawyer? And if they're anything like the lawyers I've worked with, they're expensive. Now, before she starts writing, Karen has to save up for legal fees. Brilliant!

Writers aren't the only ones who use the first kind of noble obstacle. I know some guys who say they can't work out until they pick the best exercise program. They'd hate to make a mistake and pick the wrong one. So instead they don't choose a single one because they just haven't had time to do the research.

"Until" is a hurdle you throw up on your track until the lane is so clogged you couldn't possibly get started today. Look at all those obstacles. Today's not the best day to go.

The tricky thing is that "until" often wears a cloak of responsibility. It pretends that it's not about being lazy but rather about making sure everything is in order before you start. It would be foolish to come up with a great invoice system until I really know what my business is about. Once I have a core mission, the rest of the pieces will fall into place, but until then, it would be wasted effort.

Until I know why I have an issue with food, I can't walk around the block at a brisk pace for more minutes today than I did yesterday.

Until I know what my entire book is about I can't write the first hundred words.

Until I know where all the stuff in every room of my house is going to go I can't clean this one room.

Until I pick the perfect goal I can't work on anything. That's what tripped up so many people during the 30 Days of Hustle. One participant remarked, "I honestly have so many ideas and can find justification for each of them being 'the one.' It leaves me pursuing several things at a level of mediocrity."

Until I get rid of distractions I can't get anything done. If we believe we have to eliminate all distractions before we get work done, we will never work. There will always be one more amazing distraction. Our minds will do anything to avoid the challenge of focusing on something.

The second you hear the word "until" pop into your mouth,

spit it out like Brussels sprouts that have been served without bacon. You can always tell how gross a vegetable is by how much bacon has to be added to it to do all the heavy lifting.

If . . . Then

Speaking of heavy lifting, few things are as funny as the noble obstacles used by guys who tell me they don't work out because they don't want to get "too bulky." They haven't lifted a single weight and are already worried that they'll have to start wearing those bodybuilder sweatpants from all the raw muscle they put on their frames. "I'd get fit right now but I can't afford to buy a new wardrobe. I would be drinking so many protein drinks like Fight Milk that my fast-twitch muscles would be through the roof."

These guys are deploying the second kind of noble obstacle. Instead of saying "until," they say, "if . . . then." They claim that if they pursue their goal something bad will happen. Maybe the finish will turn them into a monster. Maybe they will turn into a bad person. Either way, because they're wise and good guys, they just can't pursue their finish.

Often, the second kind of noble obstacle shows up in finances. You might decide to avoid eating healthy because if you buy healthy food you'll be poor. Everyone knows Taco Bell is a lot cheaper than anything grass fed or cage free, so because you want to be wise with your finances, you stop moving toward your goal. Or if money isn't a factor, you can always claim humility as a noble obstacle: "Pursuing a goal is a solitary activity and therefore a selfish use of my time."

You know you're employing an "if . . . then" noble obstacle if you are only offering yourself two extreme options. Either you don't work out at all or you lose so much weight you have to buy new jeans and constantly take photos standing in your old ones with the waist pulled out to show your progress. Either you don't start a business or you develop a wicked coke habit in order to stay up for twenty-two hours every day working. Either you don't sell your product or you become the most obnoxious vacuum salesperson I've ever met. Either you hold a complicated thousand-item garage sale or you don't sweep your garage floor at all. There is no in-between, just two extremes. That's the land of noble obstacles.

It's Too Hard

Remember, perfectionism has no sense of gray, things are only black or white. You do it perfectly or you don't do it at all.

Noble obstacles are why it took me so long to buy a new computer.

For the last year, I've had to delete files almost every time I use my laptop. My start-up disk is full. I'm not entirely sure what that means because usually when I get that message, my computer is too bogged down to use Google. So I just start wiping out family photos that are too heavy until Microsoft Word works again. I believe that "heavy" is the correct technological term. Sorry to go all supernerd jargon on you.

I have the money to buy a new one, but I'm a little too intimidated to walk into the Apple store. I don't know where the register is anymore. Do they have one still, or do you just buy things directly from registers mounted on the hips of geniuses? I imagine myself pacing around the brightly lit store, finally yelling at someone in a solid colored T-shirt, "I would like to buy a computer! This one!" They'll say, "Did you make a purchase appointment with our genius bar?" I'll say, "I don't know what any of those words mean. I have the money. Can I give you the money for the computer?"

They'll say, "Maybe. What are you looking for?" Only I don't know. A bigger one. A faster one. "What's your iTunes password?" they'll ask, but I don't know because I keep creating a new one every time I download an app because I forget the old one. The genius will say, "Don't worry, we can look it up with your blood type, do you know that?" I don't, I don't have any of the information he needs to make this purchase, and I can see in his eyes that they're coming out with a new, better model tomorrow. Only he won't tell me that.

If I ask him when the new model is coming out, he says "never," but that's just code for "the official release date is as soon as you complete your purchase." It might feel like today in my bones, but I'm really buying yesterday's model. I just know it. Tomorrow they'll do a press conference and release a thinner model that smells like cinnamon and has holograms and a "write my whole book automatically" button.

I'll bring what I believe is a brand-new computer to a coffee shop and people will laugh at me like I've just hitched a burro outside. That's if I can get my stuff transferred properly from the old one to the new one. Which files, programs, songs, photos, and videos do I want to move? And do I have to make that decision in the mall near the Orange Julius? I barely know this genius and now he's judging the quality of my life over the last three years based on what I'm transferring. "Don't see a lot of vacation photos in here. Not many trophies or award ceremonies either. Are your kids active? Maybe they're doing something with their lives."

I also feel like I'm rolling forward a bad storage system that I started eight years ago. It's a giant snowball of files, photos, and screenshots from 2006. Every five years I just move my junk from one storage unit to a slightly bigger storage unit. It feels similar to transferring the floating island of garbage in the Pacific Ocean to the Atlantic. Before I've used my new computer once, it's already half full of stuff I don't need.

I talked to an Apple business consultant for a minute, too. Now that I'm a business I think I'm supposed to shop that way. But I just got my LLC paperwork done a few weeks ago and I'm afraid when I say, "I'd like to buy a computer," they'll ask me what my LLC number is and I'll say, "Twelve! Was I right? Is it twelve? That's a number." It won't be, though, so I'll freak out, realizing that based on how lame my jeans are they shouldn't have even let me in this store to begin with. I'll run away, knocking over iPad Pros and geniuses/photographers/medieval history majors like so many young dominoes. I should probably talk to my lawyer who handled the LLC paperwork before I buy a computer.

I also haven't updated my OS in eighteen months. I don't know if I'm Snow Leopard or Roaring Tiger or Lazy Elephant. I just keep ignoring the "OS X Updates Available," hoping that my computer will eventually become sentient and fix itself but not kill me during the rise of Skynet.

That tangled rat's nest of complication was a Noble Obstacle for me. I didn't want to buy a new computer. I wanted to buy the perfect new computer, so instead of just hiring an IT guy to guide me through the process for a few hours, I made the whole experience as complex as possible.

I didn't want things to get easier, which is unfortunate, because that is exactly what finishers focus on.

Easy Isn't Easy but It Works

Instead of making things complicated and difficult, instead of giving in to noble obstacles, finishers stack the odds before they even start.

That phrase, "stack the odds," feels a little like cheating. Good. It should. The things we do in this book are going to continue feeling that way.

The good news is they don't have to be massive. We're not talking about shiny eureka moments. Sometimes stacking the odds is simply putting out your workout clothes the night before because at 6 A.M., you are a jerk and you will quit if you can't find socks easily in the dark. Sometimes stacking the deck is planning your important work in the morning when you're fresh and your busywork in the afternoon. Sometimes stacking the odds is buying two of your toddler's favorite stuffed animal so the world doesn't end when she inevitably leaves one at a rest stop outside of Pigeon Forge, Tennessee. Sometimes stacking the odds is just having a radiator hose.

That's what Jason Kanupp used. He made furniture in a factory in the mountains of North Carolina. For eight hours a day, he sprinted about putting couches together. He was good at it, able to complete eight couches an hour. That was how he was paid, per couch, so he was always looking for a way to stack the odds in his favor.

Over time, he noticed that the worst part of assembling a couch was twisting the legs on. In other parts of the assembly he could use tools that sped things along, but there didn't seem to be a way around the manual labor that the legs required. After some experimentation, he realized that if he attached a short piece of radiator hose, a drill bit, and a freeze plug from an engine block to a leg, he could use a power drill to screw them on. With a few simple adjustments, he cut the time it took to deal with the legs by 50 percent.

That might not seem like much, but in an average week, that trick allowed him to increase his total production by ten couches. When the company saw his innovation, they gave him a promotion and had him teach it to all the employees. I'm just kidding.

They said it wasn't fair to the other employees and made him stop. If you're looking for a new definition of bureaucracy, there it is.

Frustrated, Jason didn't quit, but instead built nineteen other radiator hose contraptions so each of his coworkers could use one, too.

Jason is a finisher, and as such, he was striving for one thing: to make things easier for himself. Starters tend to go in the opposite direction, throwing garage-sale monkey wrenches into the process.

Perfectionism always makes things harder and more complicated.

Finishers make things easier and simpler.

The next time you work on a goal, I dare you to ask the following questions during the middle of the project:

1. Could things be easier?
2. Could things be simpler?

If Bill had asked those questions, he could have come to a compromise with his wife. If he really wanted to sell some of their stuff, he could identify five items in the garage and then sell them on their neighborhood Web site.

Selling five things is a lot easier and simpler than selling an entire garage full.

And having finished that goal, he might have been ready to sell ten or even twenty next time.

If you want it done, aim for simple.

There's Still Time

Perfectionism will tell you that you've spent so long in a hiding place that there's no more time. You've missed some magical window. Your opportunity is gone. The chance has passed. Ridiculous.

In the 1970s, two writers put together a script for a movie. They pitched it as hard as they could, but no one wanted to make it. Ultimately, it sat on the shelf of some studio executive for nineteen years. Every few years, they'd dust it off and think, "Nah, it's not good."

Eventually, an agent named Tony Krantz got ahold of it. He fought for it. He pushed it up the ladder. The movie script became a TV show that eventually became the most successful drama in the history of television.

The show was called *ER*. The writers who created it almost two decades before it aired were Michael Crichton of *Jurassic Park* fame and Steven Spielberg of everything.

Nineteen years is an awful long time to sit on a shelf.

I don't know how long you've been hiding from your goal. Maybe it's nineteen days or nineteen years, the exact time doesn't really matter; the result is still the same.

Are you overfocusing on your kids because you're afraid to admit your goals matter, too?

Are you manicuring your in-box and hiding instead of working on your business plan?

Maybe you've beaten your hiding places but you've complicated your goal.

Are you tempted to learn two languages right now?

Do you ever march to the false beat of a noble obstacle?

Worrying about your book's marketing plan when you haven't even finished writing the book is a noble obstacle.

Weighing grams of carbohydrates when you haven't exercised a single minute all month is a noble obstacle.

Researching the twenty-fifth competitor in your industry when you haven't finished the LLC paperwork for your own business is a noble obstacle.

Goals are simple but they are not easy. You must leave your hiding places. You have to abandon your noble obstacles. And in perhaps the strangest way to end a chapter, you better get ready to kill some birds.

Actions:

1. Ask the three questions to identify your hiding places.
2. Share your hiding places with a friend. Give them the permission and power to tell you when they see you hiding.
3. Start creating a list of "next goals" so that you have a home for any new ideas that come up.
4. Find a hose, like Jason, our furniture builder. (Try to simplify your goal in one way.)
5. Admit and eliminate any side goals that you've taken on.
6. Ask a close friend what he or she thinks your noble obstacles are.

CHAPTER 6

Get Rid of Your Secret Rules

Most people think that the biggest jerk in the bird world is the Canada goose.

Every year, I feel like tweeting, "Dear Canada, your geese got out again. Please come get them." They're like a twenty-five-year-old son who keeps promising to get his act together soon and move out. But when you see them on a golf course, you can tell they're not working on their résumés and are probably just on Snapchat all day. They also act offended if you try to drive on a road they feel like walking across. You've got the gift of flight. Why would you ever walk anywhere?

Geese are the worst, or rather the second worst.

The biggest jerk in the bird world is undoubtedly the cuckoo.

When it's time to lay an egg, the wildly irresponsible cuckoo bird finds a nest some other bird has already built. The goal is to get another bird to raise the cuckoo so that it can focus on more reproduction. You can almost hear the mother cuckoo saying, "I don't have time to raise this baby. This kid is really getting in the way of my ability to go clubbin'." Can't you just see Maury Povich telling some bird, "You are not the father!"

The other bird species often doesn't suspect anything. The color patterns look similar and birds probably aren't good at arithmetic so the extra egg goes unnoticed.

The cuckoo bird has a faster incubation rate so it tends to hatch first. Know what the first thing it does is? Kill the other birds. Using sharp mandibles and probably discouraging words, it crushes the other eggs. If the other birds have already hatched, the cuckoo throws its nestmates out while the mother is foraging for food.

Imagine, you're a mother bird, you've just caught a worm for your four children. You fly home, already pretty mad that the father of these children is who knows where, and suddenly there are only three birds in the nest. That's weird, you think to yourself, I swear I had four kids, and why is one so much huskier than the others?

One by one, your kids die in some sort of avian *Game of Thrones* situation. Eventually feeding a species much larger than yourself proves too exhausting. As you take your last tiny, bird breath, a huge cuckoo looms over you and says, "Thank you," like when Kylo Ren killed his father, Han Solo. Come on, you had eighteen months to see that movie. That spoiler is on you.

The frustrating thing is that it doesn't have to end that way for the mother bird. Some birds recognize that a new egg has been placed in the nest. Some will throw the cuckoo bird out, or weave a nest on top of it so that it dies, or refuse to sit on it so that it never develops. They break the parasitic cycle and raise a happy bird family without that cuckoo jerk ruining everything.

Once I learned the terrible truth about cuckoo birds, I started punching every clock I saw. I'd wait until noon, standing right next to the elaborate wooden cuckoo clock Thomas Kinkade fans still own. As soon as it came out I'd swing the most precise punch you've ever seen. The trick is to crumple the bird without destroying the clock. I'm great at it now, but like most forms of expertise it took about ten thousand hours to perfect. I'm no longer allowed in antique stores in Middle Tennessee.

How do you not notice your home has been invaded by a dangerous parasite? How do you miss the lie? The same way most of us carry secret rules for how we're supposed to live our lives. That's the brilliance of perfectionism.

At the core, perfectionism is a desperate attempt to live up to impossible standards. We wouldn't play if we knew the whole game was impossible, so perfectionism promises us that we just need to follow some secret rules. As long as we do that, perfect is possible. So over the years, as you chase goals, perfectionism quietly adds some secret rules to your life.

Like the one that told Rob O'Neill, "Wheels don't count."

When he accepted a high-powered position as a Viacom vice president, Rob purchased new luggage for all the travel he'd be doing.

He bought expensive leather bags befitting an executive of his stature. As is often the case with luxury items, the bags were high on form and low on function. The leather was heavy and the carry strap cut into his shoulder. For months he jetted between Los Angeles and New York, grimacing uncomfortably but convinced that that was just the way things had to be.

One night, while waiting for a connection in Atlanta, he saw a fellow business traveler who didn't look as strained as he felt. On the contrary, she was sharply dressed and practically gliding through the terminal on the way to her next meeting. Beside her she easily rolled a suitcase. She even looked peaceful, which is saying something at the Atlanta airport, because most of the employees there hate you. In that moment, Rob asked himself, "Why don't I think wheels count?" He'd never said that rule out loud, but some part of him had decided that using wheels was cheating. Travel had to be difficult. It had to be painful. It had to be frustrating.

That week he ordered a suitcase with wheels and never looked back.

Somewhere along the way, he'd internalized the idea that it was cheating to use wheels. It wasn't just wheels, though. The bigger rule was "For something to count, it has to be difficult." A lot of high performers carry that sort of secret rule along with them. If an exercise is enjoyable and you have fun doing it, it must not count.

Joy then becomes a good indicator that you're not working hard enough or making enough progress.

Pull that thread far enough and you end up with the rule "If I'm not miserable, I'm not doing something productive."

That's as crazy as a small bird not recognizing there's a gigantic bird in its nest that looks nothing like every other baby they've ever had. (This is like the ugly duckling who grew up to be a swan, except in this fairy tale the swan murders everyone.)

You've got some secret rules that make it really difficult for you to finish.

I do, too.

One of mine is "If it doesn't come easily, it's not worth doing." Another way to say it is "If you have to learn something new, you're failing."

I had a fast start at a few things in life. In 2008, for instance, I started a blog that went viral. Nine days after I launched it, four thousand people showed up to read it. That was a really fun experience, but the rule I took away was "If something hasn't blown up by Day 10, it's a failure." I'm prone to give up on projects as soon as they don't deliver an avalanche of positive results.

For years, I've had a nest full of cuckoos chirping out secret rules. They look roughly like the other thoughts in my head, but the more I listen to them and feed them, the more the truth gets starved.

After close to ten years of believing that one rule, it's incredibly difficult for me to learn something new. I feel ashamed if I have to ask someone a question. I feel embarrassed if I have to admit I don't know how to do something. I fake my way through a lot of life, believing that learning is failing. Real winners don't have to learn. They just know already.

The worst part is that by nature, I am an enthusiastic learner.

Every personality test on the planet shouts out that I like to experience new things. But my nest is full of secret rules, and the longer I live with them, the bigger they become.

I'm not alone in that particular rule either. Jet fighters apparently struggle with it as well, which is yet one more example of how I'm similar to a jet fighter. Jeff Orr is an F-16 flight instructor who works with some of the best fighter pilots in the nation. Sometimes, young pilots try to rush through the 100-point checklist that goes into each flight. "Some pilots go fast to show you they know what they're doing. They're afraid to work hard because then it won't seem authentic or natural."

Another secret rule I live my life by is "Success is bad."

My dad is a pastor and I grew up on the outside of money. I remember him telling me a number of times that if anyone ever gave him a nice luxury car, he would give it back. It was just melted metal and plastic. We were miles away from living in poverty, but there was definitely a sense that it was somehow sinful to be successful.

My dad probably doesn't even remember those few offhand comments he made about wealth and success, but it's surprisingly easy for the smallest comment to turn into a cuckoo, or what psychiatrists call a limiting belief. Thirty years after I started believing that success was bad, I found myself passing on that limiting belief to my oldest daughter.

Mike Posner is a musician who had a huge hit with a song called "Cooler than Me." He wrote the song as a college student and was surprised by the rocket ride it took him on. It wasn't an easy ride, though, as captured in the song he released six years later, describing what it's like to be considered a one-hit wonder. In "I Took a Pill in Ibiza," he sings:

I'm just a singer who already blew his shot.
I get along with old timers,
Cause my name's a reminder of a pop song people forgot.

Hidden inside this happy, infectious pop song is an honest look at what can happen in the record industry.

I told my daughter about it and then forgot we ever had that conversation until one day in the car.

The song came on and I heard her remark to her friend, "This song is about a guy who had a hit and the fame destroyed him." She might have used the word "fame," but I could recognize the start of a cuckoo. Success will destroy you. Success is dangerous. Success is to be avoided.

I never said those things to my daughter. My dad never said those things to me either. But cuckoos don't need much to grow bigger than you could ever imagine.

In my own life, the last eight years have been a bit difficult because of that particular lie. I'm not alone in this, as there are many people who struggle with a fear of success. The more successful they get, the guiltier they get, too.

A friend at a dinner party once told me, "That CEO of the

health-care company makes twenty million dollars a year. I wonder how he sleeps at night?"

I wanted to respond, "Probably peacefully on a comforter made of Hungarian down." He clearly thought success was bad, and that after you've made a certain arbitrary amount of income, you were no longer able to sleep well. What's that line? If you make $5 million, you're able to sleep at night, but no longer have access to Sunday afternoon naps out of guilt?

This cuckoo ends up being a double-edged sword. If I fail, it hurts because failing isn't fun. If I win, I feel ashamed of the success and that hurts. It's the very picture of lose-lose.

That's how you know you're dealing with a cuckoo, when either outcome makes you unhappy. Rob's back and shoulder hurt lugging around difficult suitcases, but using one with wheels made him feel like a failure. There was no middle ground.

I can teach you a million strategies and tricks, but if you're bringing them home to a nest chock-full of parasites, none of it matters.

To deal with our secret rules, we have to do three things:

1. Identify them.
2. Destroy them.
3. Replace them.

Let's start with figuring out what they are.

Four Questions to Smoke Out Your Secret Rules

The problem with secret rules is that they're secret. They're often buried deep inside, hidden by years and years of misbelief. You don't even know you're following them.

That friend of yours who has a terrible boyfriend she has been engaged to for nine years? She believes the secret rule that she doesn't deserve better. That family member who hates his job but doesn't feel qualified for anything else? His secret rule tells him he's lucky anyone would hire him at all.

Call it baggage, call it limiting beliefs, call it secret rules—the name doesn't matter. The results do, and it would be useless to teach you a thousand ways to finish when your secret rule is going to trip you five feet from the finish line every time.

To really smoke out your secret rules, I want you to ask yourself these four questions:

1. Do I even like _____?

One of perfectionism's favorite secret rules is "Only miserable, difficult goals count." This is the rule that drives every person who jogs to lose weight when they would really rather be doing Zumba, but it's not just exercise where we see this rule at play. It rears its head in our career choices as well. Being a weatherman is not an easy job. In addition to the fickle nature of weather and the data you must interpret, there aren't that many positions available. In any given city, there are less than a dozen job openings for on-air weather talent. Once one weather expert is beloved at a TV station, they often stay on board for decades, effectively preventing other people from advancing up the ladder. Charlie Neese knew how lucky he was to have a job in Nashville and had made a great name for himself over the years. He liked sharing the weather with viewers, but he started to realize he didn't like a lot of the other responsibilities. It was difficult to miss his son's football games because he was working each weekend. Manning the weather desk at night and into the early morning made it difficult to connect with his wife as well. But no one leaves a great job, especially in a popular market like Nashville. The more Charlie asked the question, "Do I even like being a meteorologist?" though, the more the answer came up "No." He eventually left the station, despite the shock of coworkers and fans, and became a real estate agent. His family is happy, he's happy, and he's great at his new job. How do I know? He sold our house in a matter of days. Don't wait to be honest with yourself if you realize you no longer like what you're working on. Don't let perfectionism keep you stuck.

2. What's my real goal?

Rob's real goal for his luggage was to travel comfortably. As a successful fifty-year-old executive, impressing strangers with his suitcases didn't really matter to him. But as we discussed, perfectionism loves to distract us, and what better way than confusing your real goal with some fake secret rules. During the research for this book, secret rules kept coming to the surface, especially around weight-loss goals. One woman told me, "There was this number I was constantly chasing and it drove me crazy." Her secret rule that she wasn't successful unless she met that number goal haunted her for so long that she finally gave up and had to figure out what she really wanted. The number wasn't what she wanted. "I wanted health. I wanted to prevent diabetes, heart disease, and everything else my mother was taking medication for. That forced me to be honest about my own health, which then forced me to research how to reverse some damage I had done." Getting to the heart of the goal allowed her to connect her heart to the results. The weight came off as she worked on changing bad habits into good ones.

If you're not excited about your goal right now, ask yourself, "What's my real goal?" Make sure that what you're chasing is actually what you want to catch. As you progress with your goal you should continue to come back to this gut-check question because it's really easy to get off track despite your best intentions.

Kristi Duggins succinctly captures what can happen along the way by describing how she felt when her goal morphed into a business. "I love making things. I started an Etsy shop. It went really well. I started hating making things. Closed my shop. Back to enjoying the things now." Kristi's secret rule was that you must sell the things you create. Simply making them wasn't enough. What's fascinating about that is that her goal didn't fail. It wasn't failure that made it hard to hang on to the heart of what her real goal was—it was success. The store didn't just go well, it went "really well." Whether you hit potholes or whatever is the positive, opposite version of a pothole (*The Dukes of Hazzard* jumpable dirt pile?), don't let your true north get away from you. What's fun about this approach is that knowing what your real goal is opens you up to a wide variety of methods to accomplish it. Instead of narrowly thinking you must write a memoir because that's your rule, when your goal is "share your art," there are a thousand ways you can finish that.

3. Does the method I'm using match who I am?

A very common secret rule is "What I'm naturally talented at doesn't count." If something comes easily or comfortably, it must not be good. Why does perfectionism offer up this rule? Because if things that come naturally are cheating, then you're doomed to pursue difficult goals you're sure to quit. It's like telling a fish to travel a nautical mile without swimming. At the beginning of this book I confessed that I only finished 6 days in the 90-day P90X program. It would be easy to assume that using the shortcuts in this book I went back and finished the 84 other days. The truth is that although the principles have helped me finish a lot more often, I will never complete that program. It's not because I'm lazy, it's because I'm community driven. I like group exercise. I like the accountability of being part of a class. I like the comradery of getting up early and knowing other people are, too. I like having my workout planned by an expert who barks motivational statements at me when I feel like quitting. I like the friendly competition I get by working out with friends. I thought I was a failure when it comes to exercise because I didn't finish P90X, but it turns out I was just using the wrong method. When I joined Orangetheory, an hour-long circuit training class with some friends, I got in great shape. I go with guys from my neighborhood. Accountability? Check. You wear a heart-rate monitor during class, with all your vital stats shown on TVs that everyone can see. Competition? Check. A trainer guides you through each exercise, pushing you to do better. Motivation? Check. It hits every one of my buttons and consequently I've gone consistently for the last twelve months. The P90X program is amazing, but I'm not built to be the guy who works out alone in his living room with no feedback whatsoever. At the same time, my friend Jason is wrapping up his third round of P90X. That's the method that works for him. If you don't have a lot of joy in your goal right now, make sure you're using a method that plays to your strengths. If you pursue the right goal in the wrong way, you still end up in the wrong place.

4. Is it time to quit?

"Winners never quit!" might look good on a poster, but it's actually a lie and a dangerous secret rule. The truth is, there are some things you can't learn until you try them. You might need to run a month or two before you decide if you like it. You might need to try writing a novel for a while before you can accurately tell if there's any joy. You might need to put together a business plan to get a sense of what's really involved in opening a spice shop in your town. When you do, though, you'll face the challenge of figuring out if it's something you really enjoy. The middle of any goal is difficult and uncomfortable. How do you know if what you're experiencing is genuine displeasure because you picked the wrong goal, or just the normal frustration that comes with the middle part of a goal?

Laura Murphy-Rizk faced that question in law school. Being a lawyer was her dream, and she had some incredibly noble reasons. She wanted to become a lobbyist so that she could help change cancer legislation, funding, and research. Her grandmother, aunt, and three cousins died before the age of fifty. "I felt like if I didn't make it happen, I was letting my family down, too." She went to law school for three semesters, "but the truth was I hated every waking moment of it. My grip was so tight to the dream that I was making myself, and everyone else around me, miserable." A lot of pressure comes with picking a career. It's a big goal that often gets tangled up with family expectations. Laura eventually quit and ten years later is a lot happier for it. One of perfectionism's favorite secret rules is "Winners never quit." Of course they do—people quit stupid things regularly. At times like that, it's important to get wise counsel from people you know and trust. We're often so wrapped up in our secret rules that we have a hard time seeing that quitting might be the best option for us. Finishing a goal you absolutely hate isn't a win.

Spend a few minutes honestly answering these questions. It's not the easiest exercise in the book because some of your secret rules might have been ingrained for years. Perhaps you believed your dad when he told you that your creative arts major would never make money. Maybe an ex-boyfriend made an offhand comment about your looks that mutated into a secret rule you still live with every time you look in the mirror. Or maybe you're believing a very common secret rule that says your work doesn't count unless you do it alone.

Borrow Someone Else's Diploma

As I mentioned earlier, one of perfectionism's chief goals is to isolate you. It's easier to get you to believe lies and follow secret rules when you don't have a community telling you the truth and calling you out on your rules.

In order to separate you from the herd, perfectionism will tell you a very popular secret rule: "You have to do it all on your own."

This always reminds me of toddlers. They'd rather fall down a flight of stairs than hold your hand, because they want to do it "all by my big self!"

We become adult toddlers when we refuse help from people and believe the lie that seeking assistance is a sign of weakness.

Author Jessica Turner doesn't feel that way though. When she was going to do a Webinar for a sales team I had done a Webinar for, she called and interviewed me. I had learned a lot and made some mistakes. For instance, if you want people to show up at your Webinar, you have to e-mail them twice on the day of, three hours before and then five minutes before it starts. Did you know that? I sure didn't, until I learned it from Lewis Howes. I tried it and it dramatically increased attendance at the next Webinar I did. I passed that on to Jessica. If you don't have any information of your own, someone else does and will give it to you if you ask the right way.

I call this "borrowing someone else's diploma," and it isn't a particularly new technique. Actor Will Smith did it decades ago, and he probably owes the IRS a thank-you for that.

When he was nineteen years old and touring the country as a rapper, the department asked him for $2.8 million. I don't know if that's done via a phone call, letter, or a reverse Ed McMahon big check with balloons, but that's definitely a frightening day for a teenager.

It wasn't a donation the IRS was looking for but back taxes. Smith didn't come from money. His divorced parents were middle class, with his dad working seven days a week to run a refrigerator company and his mother employed by the school board. A run-in with the IRS would have crippled most people, but Smith started gathering new information in the midst of that season.

Two years later, as he got ready to move to L.A. from West

Philadelphia born and raised for his first acting gig, his manager, James Lassiter, approached him. "Listen, if we're going out to L.A., we probably should have a goal." The transition from rapper to actor would not happen by accident. "I want to be the biggest movie star in the world," Smith replied.

That sentence in and of itself isn't that unique. A thousand people riding buses from the Midwest out to Hollywood say that every week. Smith also had very little evidence that it would work. He wasn't a blockbuster actor yet. He was a twenty-one-year-old rapper whose biggest hit at the time had been a PG-flavored rap called "Parents Just Don't Understand." It's not just the goal that separates Smith from other would-be superstars. It's what happened next.

Lassiter did some research and came up with a list of the ten top-grossing movies of all time. This was not difficult. Someone had already been the world's biggest star. "We looked at them and said, O.K., what are the patterns?" Smith said.

"We realized that ten out of ten had special effects. Nine out of ten had special effects with creatures. Eight out of ten had special effects with creatures and a love story."

That seems too simple to work, right?

There's no way you can plan a twenty-five-year film career, in the ficklest industry in the world, with a top-ten list that everyone has access to. That's not sophisticated enough. It needs to be more difficult than that. Or so we think, until we see the list of Will Smith's six most successful movies.

1. *Independence Day*: Special effects, creatures, love story; $817 million worldwide lifetime gross.
2. *Suicide Squad*: Special effects, creatures, love story; $746 million worldwide lifetime gross.
3. *Hancock*: Special effects. $624 million worldwide lifetime gross.
4. *Men in Black 3*: Special effects, creatures, love story; $624 million worldwide lifetime gross.
5. *Men in Black*: Special effects, creatures, love story; $589 million lifetime gross.
6. *I Am Legend*: Special effects, creatures (love story if you count the dog); $585 million lifetime gross.

Why does Smith believe in the power of borrowing someone else's diploma? He has 4 billion reasons.

Does doing this guarantee success? Nope. *Wild Wild West* was a Wild Wild bust. But in most goals it's not about winning all the time, it's about winning more than you lose. We're not aiming for perfection. All you have to do is win more today than you did yesterday and repeat the whole thing tomorrow. If six of the twenty-four movies you star in make more than $4 billion, you get to make more movies for a very long time, even if some of them flop.

Don't ever accept the secret rule that you have to go it alone. Don't let perfectionism isolate you.

Find someone with an amazing diploma and then borrow it.

Knowing Is Only Half the Battle

Knowing what your secret rules are is a great start to this conversation but it's not the conclusion.

What do you do once you've identified them? What's the best next step?

It's time to destroy them.

The first thing you should do is simply ask the question, "What does that mean?" for each secret rule you encounter.

For example, if I wrote down the rule "Success is bad," under that I would write down the question "What does that mean?"

Then I'd have to answer it.

I'd say, "Success is bad, which must mean that failure is good. To fail is the best. Winning is terrible and the only way I'll know I'm doing good is to fail. If I can lose money, gain cheese weight, and crash my car, I'll be having a pretty baller year."

Those are stupid sentences right there, but that's the goal. You want to see how ridiculous your fake rule really is.

Perfectionism persists unless we ask questions. A well-phrased question is a burst of water at a dam we need to break. It's looking at the impossible standard we've been living against and picking it apart. It's like peeking behind the curtain in *The Wizard of Oz*. With the smoke and the thunder and the production, it seems like there really might be a giant of a warlord behind the whole operation. But if we were to ask a few questions, we might find out there's just a feeble, scared old man running the show.

The second question to ask is "Who says?" You'd be amazed at how many cuckoos this question takes care of. In a lot of situations, the answer is going to be "nobody." No one says it has to be as difficult as you're making it, but when we believe a cuckoo we act as if some authority has made it so.

Sometimes, the origin of the "who says" goes deeper because perfectionism is often a team sport. You'll hear successful people admit they work so hard because they're trying to prove to their father that they're good enough. In many cases, the father passed away years ago and they're arguing with a ghost. If they stopped and asked, "Who says?" they'd realize that killing themselves for someone who would never know about it was fruitless.

A friend had a difficult time being present in her marriage because her mom told her that her independence was the only thing that mattered. Her mom had been divorced and lost everything, so the secret rule she passed on was "Never be vulnerable enough to get hurt." My friend could love her husband, but only up until the line that told her she was giving too much. When she asked, "Who says?" she realized she was living her life out of her mom's fear.

The third step to getting rid of a secret rule is to write a new rule to replace it.

Mine would be "Success is good."

Yours might be "I can be in shape and still be modest." That might sound funny, but that's what Ingrid Griffin struggled with. She said, "I sabotage my physical goals because 'skinny is slutty' and being just a little chunky is 'more humble.'"

She is very well aware how insane that is. Can you imagine sitting down to a Big Mac and silently telling yourself, "I am so humble. It's the secret sauce that really holds the most humility. Ranch dressing is the least arrogant of all the salad dressings."

Write down your secret rules. Answer the question "What does that mean?" and then write yourself a new rule, a flexible, reasonable, healthy rule based on the truth.

The Head and the Heart

I've read more books about goals than I've accomplished actual goals. That's probably a sign of something. Something not good.

The problem with a lot of the books is that they only deal with the head. They tell you mechanical things you should do and treat you like an unfeeling robot who will march through each goal with efficiency and practicality. They don't take into account the secret rules we're harboring in our hearts, rules that our brains have often never consciously evaluated.

They don't take into account that you've convinced yourself that being in shape is slutty.

That's an absolutely crazy rule, but welcome to the heart side of things, where we often accept damaging judgments because of our past.

Rob O'Neill manages tens of millions of dollars for Viacom, but didn't think he was allowed to own a comfortable suitcase.

That's an absolutely crazy rule, but welcome to the heart side of things, where perfectionism tricks us into making life hard for ourselves.

For years, my kids begged me to write them a story, but I thought I couldn't write a story unless I illustrated it as well.

That's an absolutely crazy rule. You know what I'm not? An illustrator, and I never finished. Welcome to the heart side of things, where our perfectionism keeps us from blessing people we love.

Our heads are often not aware of our heart's secret rules, rules that perfectionism has etched into us. If we don't examine ourselves mindfully and gently, we may think that our failures to meet our goals are due to our laziness or bad strategy, when in reality they are caused by the secret rules that make our finishes impossible.

Is it a coincidence that "cuckoo" is another word for "crazy"? Probably not. These rules sound insane, and they will drive you insane if you don't deal with them.

Kill yours today. They're doing damage to your heart. Your goal will be a whole lot easier if you're not listening to secret rules. You'll actually have room in your life for what we're going to gather next.

Actions:

1. Listen for a few secret rules and write them down. (This will take longer than one sitting since you're asking your head to Google something that might be hidden.)

2. Write the truth next to each secret rule. To find it, ask "What does that mean" and "Who says?"

3. Create a new rule to replace the old one.

4. Enlist a friend to help you see when you're living by a secret rule.

CHAPTER 7

Use Data to Celebrate
Your Imperfect Progress

Aweek after Easter, I asked my friend who works at a church how the service went. Easter is like the Super Bowl for churches. His answer surprised me.

"It was good. The music was great. We had a solid turnout, but we lost a few animals."

"What do you mean, you lost a few animals? Like they went on a *Homeward Bound* journey with Michael J. Fox voicing one of them?" I replied.

"No, we had a few animals die."

For Easter, my friend's church decided to have a petting zoo, just like they did in the Bible. Unfortunately, church volunteers might be good at helping you find an empty seat, but they're terrible at running makeshift zoos.

The first animal to go was a rabbit. Apparently, a three-year-old did a suplex off a hay bale and landed on the rabbit. The truth is, rabbits have really tiny bones. They're also not good at wrestling. They're good at one physical activity, but not so good at any others.

The second animal to go home to see Jesus that Easter was a duck. A little kid hugged the duck too hard, in the neck. What do you do in that moment? Do you give the lifeless duck to the family, kind of like the craft for that morning? Cover it in a thin layer of glitter and voila, "Here's your duck"?

My friend didn't need to be told those two moments were failures. He was well aware that they missed the mark. That's the funny thing about failure. It's loud. You might never lose a duck on your watch, but you know when you've blown it.

Progress, on the other hand, is quiet. It whispers. Perfectionism screams failure and hides progress.

That's the reason a little data can make a big difference. It helps you see through perfectionism's claims that you're not getting anywhere and helps you celebrate your achievements.

Without data, progress virtually disappears. The problem is what I call the "candle effect."

When you light a candle in a pitch-black room without windows, the effects are dramatic. Going from complete dark to light is substantial progress. The difference is obvious and immediately felt. Lighting a second candle has a big effect, too, albeit not as big. The third candle is still impressive, but not as impressive. This diminishing continues until the impact of a new candle is hardly noticed. The fifteenth candle would barely register on your brightness scale.

We want our goals to have compounding interest, not diminishing returns. We hope that with each passing accomplishment, the progress will grow and momentum will build, but that's rarely how things go.

Take running, for instance. The candle effect comes into play with mile times. If you work hard and increase your speed from 3 miles per hour to 4 miles per hour you'll move from a 20-minute mile to a 15-minute mile. That's massive progress and all you did was increase the speed by 1 mile per hour. If, however, you improve from 9 miles per hour to 10 miles per hour, you don't cut 5 minutes from your per mile time. You cut 40 seconds. The rate of improvement drops by more than 80 percent.

The same goes with eating well. Let's say you want to eat healthy for six days a week and take one cheat day. That would mean, in a standard meal plan, you have to eat well for eighteen meals every week. When you eat the first meal well, you're one eighteenth done. The second makes you one ninth done. The third makes you one sixth done. What progress! But the higher you get in the count, the less dramatic the progress gets. Whether you're thirteen meals in or fourteen meals in doesn't really move the scale much. The big gains are gone.

Perfectionism uses these shrinking levels of success as proof that things aren't going well. Remember, in the middle of a goal, perfectionism is trying to convince you that the results aren't good enough and that you should quit. What better way to discourage you than to point out your glacial progress?

Why do I want you to have a few points of data? Because

when perfectionism gets loud in the middle of your goal, I want a piece of paper with the truth on it.

Perfectionism hates data. Why? Because emotions lie, data doesn't.

Our emotions will give us a completely false impression of a given situation.

How do I know? Has every worry you've ever had come true? Have all the fears and anxieties you've had come to fruition? Was it helpful that your brain kept you awake at night thinking about something stupid you said four years ago? Did every failure you were concerned about come to bear on your life?

Of course not. In the middle of the night, your emotions got you spinning. Over and over you worked through the reason your boss said she wants to talk to you tomorrow. It's never a good thing; it's only dire.

In moments like that, our emotions get riled up and tell us wild stories.

Not data.

Data cuts through all the noise.

It cuts through all the clutter.

It cuts through all the distractions and hype and hopelessness and anything else that's in your way right now.

In its wake it leaves you with everything you need to make a good decision for tomorrow.

That's all data is. A gift from yesterday that you receive today to make tomorrow better.

To make the most of the data, we need to understand how it can help us, why we hate it, and how to use it.

Data Moves Us Beyond Discouragement

Jason Bartlett wants to lose forty pounds. A sedentary job as a pharmacist made it easy to pack on some sneaky pounds. He knew he was carrying around more weight than he wanted to, but Thanksgiving is what really pushed him over the edge. Well, not Thanksgiving exactly, but his wife's grandmother. As he entered her room at the nursing home, Grandma Betsy looked up from her book and announced simply, "Well, Jason got fat." Old people and little kids tell the truth. We only act polite in between.

Although forty pounds seems like a lot—Jason was after all trying to lose a kindergartner—it wasn't impossible because he had done it before. Like most dieters, this was not his first attempt.

Unfortunately, at forty-four, he was finding those extra pounds persistent. They were refusing to leave despite eight weeks of hard work. He hired a personal trainer. He was running more. He was being careful about what he ate, and every morning the scale refused to budge an inch.

This is the moment when most people bother to first review the progress. When the goal is taking too long, when the desired outcome is playing hide-and-seek, we peek up from our work in dismay.

The diet is not working. The promotion is not coming. The book is not spilling out on the pages at the clip you'd prefer.

Perfectionism will point that out and suggest that now might be a good time to give up. This was a stupid goal anyway. Why did I want to finish that in the first place? I'm not making perfect progress, so I must not be doing anything. We give up because we do not review the progress the right way.

When things aren't going well, it's not time to give up. It's time to get your bearings and make adjustments. "Adjustments?!" perfectionism screams. "If you need to adjust, you might as well give up!" Don't listen. It's time to look at your GPS watch and see how your pace is. It's time to read the course markers and make sure you're still headed to the finish line. It's time to adjust the next few miles based on what you learned about your pace from the first few miles.

If I were on the side of the course, watching all the runners, I might yell out to you, "How's the race going?"

If you answered, "No idea! I don't know how fast I'm going, how many miles I have left, or even which way to go. I'm just going to run faster to fix that problem, though," I would think you are dumb.

If you don't review the progress, you can't make adjustments. You can't learn from mistakes. You can't get better, and ultimately, you can't finish.

Perfectionism doesn't want you to look at the progress. It might tell you that you don't need to. Smarter people don't need maps or measurements or data. Or it might tell you that you'll be afraid of what you'll find. For a solid year, I didn't look at my book sales data because I was scared of what I would learn. At the most extreme edge of this problem are people who refuse to go to the doctor because they're afraid to find out they might be seriously sick.

For a thousand reasons, this doesn't make any sense.

We laugh at hamsters stuck on their metal play wheels. They give everything their little hamster bodies have but don't go anywhere. That doesn't matter, though, because they have little hamster brains. The hamster isn't trying to finish anything. If anything he's just trying to execute that elusive move where you get the wheel going so fast that you can do a full 360 around the circle. I bet the girl hamsters love that.

You are smarter than a hamster. There's a positive affirmation for you. Slap that on a mug.

You might not be on a wheel, but if you ignore where you're headed, you probably will get discouraged and not finish.

Never Play Golf at Night

Jason's frustration with his slow progress toward losing forty pounds was fake. He was legitimately frustrated, but the cause of it was vapor. He was disappointed because the previous time he lost weight it had felt so easy. The pounds had come off quickly. It wasn't as hard as this time.

Only he doesn't have any data to back that up, only memories and feelings and the chirping of perfectionism. He didn't keep track of the effort he expended last time. He didn't have any real information to review. Study after study has shown that eyewitness accounts can be incredibly sketchy. Mere moments after a violent crime, bystanders will remember the guy definitely had a mustache. Or he definitely didn't. He was tall and wearing a long black coat. Or he was short and didn't have a coat on at all.

Our memories are constantly editing themselves and therefore are unreliable. Feelings are not much better. Chances are, the first time he lost that weight, it was very difficult. There were hard moments where he fought for another breath on an exercise bike. The scale didn't always show results that time either. But his feelings tell another story.

If someone can't accurately remember a moment like a robbery a day after it happened, why do we trust our memories of events that occurred months or years ago?

If Jason had taken more points of data than just the scale, he could quiet the doubtful voice of perfectionism that crept into his progress review.

Here are data points he missed:

Pants size
Shirt size
BMI
Number of times he jogged
Number of miles he ran

Number of times he worked with the trainer

Food diary

Some of those data points would have shown progress, like pants size, while others would have proved process, like number of times he ran.

But like most people who try to finish something, he didn't leave himself enough data points for the future.

Since you decided to gather some data, though, let's discuss what will happen when you review it, or why you should never play golf at night.

My favorite thing about golf is not playing.

Currently, I play once every two years, or whenever we have Thanksgiving with my wife's family. One time I lost nineteen balls during a round of eighteen holes. Jenny's uncle now brings me sacks of range balls that have been removed from the bottom of lagoons to play with.

Last year he didn't bring me a bag of clubs to borrow, just a handful of irons zip-tied as if they'd been taken hostage at a sporting goods store. Is there anything classier than showing up at a country club and handing the cart guy your fistful of zip-tied clubs? Careful with this, son; that's one of my best zip ties.

I'm not good at golf and you'd stink, too, if you only practiced at night. Journalist Matthew Syed noted in his book *Black Box Thinking: Why Most People Never Learn from Their Mistakes— But Some Do* what a bad plan playing at night is if you want to get better. He writes, "Suppose that instead of practicing in daylight, you practice at night—in the pitch-black. In these circumstances, you could practice for ten years or ten thousand years without improving at all. How could you progress if you don't have a clue where the ball has landed? . . . You wouldn't have any data to improve your accuracy."

We'd all judge people who play golf at night, well, judge and not give them our real phone numbers. That's a Google Voice opportunity right there.

The reason we'd find them so foolish is that for all their playing, they'd never get better. They could spend every night out there in the dark trying to play perfectly, and it wouldn't improve their game because as soon as the ball left the tee, it would disappear.

Most of us chase our goals this same way. The minute some action we've taken has left our hands, it's gone, lost somewhere in the busyness of the day.

How many inches have we lost during our diet? What percent of body fat? How many hours did we work out this week versus last week? How much has our salary grown over the last three years? How many total words did we write this summer versus last? How many dollars do we have saved up for our next vacation? Is our progress on this goal any different from the last goal?

Do you think it's accidental that casinos don't put clocks on the walls or use a lot of windows in their designs? They know that if they remove that bit of data, you'll be more likely to play longer. Without knowing the time or that the day has become night, it's easy to get lost in the action. Even their motto hints at perfectionism. "What happens in Vegas stays in Vegas." As if you could have a disastrous weekend in Vegas and have your real life back home remain perfect without any consequences from the trip.

When you play golf in the dark, you're prone to make a lot of mistakes.

One Friday, my team launched the sales of a new online course. It was the first day people could buy it and we had twelve hundred people on the early sign-up list. That meant we could e-mail more than a thousand people who had directly expressed interest in this course. Those were what you call "warm leads" in sales terms.

Knowing those numbers, what kind of response would you expect? Let's guess at some data, since that's usually what you have to do when you're golfing at night without any real numbers. If we sold the course to 10 percent of the audience, that would mean 120 people would sign up. Maybe that's too aggressive, though; 5 percent would still mean 60 people. I started to run the numbers and got really excited about the possibilities. Fortunately, data came to the rescue.

My social media guy, Bryan Allain, texted me and said, "Just as a reminder, we've never seen better than 0.4% conversion on our Friday sneak peek e-mails. Our initial launch was our best, 55 sales on 13,900 e-mails. Feb was 16 sales, May was 26, September was 11. So by those numbers we should expect 5 sales today with our 1,200-person launch."

That text message kept me off the ledge when we ended up selling only four courses that day. Without the data, I might have thought we were failing. I would have grown discouraged at the terrible turnout. Instead, with some data, I knew we were right on track. I didn't let perfectionism tell me the failure was a disaster.

Data tells the truth and makes things a lot easier. So why don't we use it?

Data Is the Worst

If you don't check your bank account, you won't see how low it is and won't feel bad. So the solution to feeling good is to ignore your bank account. And the scale. And your doctor. And your crazy-crowded-with-junk garage. And the issues in your marriage.

As we said earlier, perfectionism is a desperate attempt to live up to impossible standards. Perfectionism will do anything to protect those impossible standards. It can't let you find out how impossible they are, especially with the cold eye of data, so it terrifies you into thinking that you'll be crushed by disappointment if you peer behind that curtain.

Data would tell you that your bank account is low, but you're spending a lot more on coffee than you think. If you started making it at home, you could easily start saving for a vacation. You might even stop comparing yourself to the impossible financial standards of your friends online. You might make some reasonable goals and completely change the way you view money. You might even have fun.

Perfectionism hated that entire paragraph.

Better to tell you that if you step on the scale, you'll be crushed by the weight you've gained instead of admitting a little data received, but not obsessed on, goes a long way toward changing things. Perfectionism would much rather you have some crazy magazine-cover body as your goal. I love when the picture is a six foot two model and a headline that says, "HOW I GOT THIS BODY!" The article never mentions, "Well, my parents are both six foot three and I have to admit that helped with the whole long leg thing, but maybe you should do more squats."

Data would tell us the truth and perfectionism can't stand the truth. That's why we hate data, because for years perfectionism has demonized it.

I can't stand it. I would rather ignore it. I'd rather speed my way down a highway that might contain a bridge that is out instead of actually deal with what data is trying to tell me.

Data is not fun. Data is not sexy. Data is not my friend.

Or so I thought and so most of us think.

It's way more enjoyable to ignore it and feign surprise at where our lives take us than it is to be deliberate about listening to the data and responding appropriately. Even that word "appropriately" feels boring.

A lot of our problems in life are self-inflicted and not mysteries. If you smoke, you have a much greater chance of getting lung cancer. If you spend all your time at work on Facebook, you're probably not going to get a promotion. If you eat Taco Bell multiple times a week, all the running in the world won't help.

That last one stings a bit. Have you ever ordered so much Taco Bell that the sack it's in set off the seat belt alarm when placed next to you in the car? That's probably a sign I should not ignore, but I can't help myself when I go to that restaurant. It's the only fast-food place where I get confused by the menu and order multiple items. I don't make that mistake at McDonald's. I never say, "I'll have a quarter pounder with cheese and a side of Big Mac!" But at Taco Bell, all bets are off as I traipse through that à la carte menu gathering items like a Tex-Mex snowball rolling down a seven-layer burrito hill.

So upon plopping down the bag one day in the passenger seat—nobody puts baby in the corner—the alarm started chirping. "Careful, something heavy enough to be considered a human is now in the seat. Please buckle it in."

I laughed at my rental Kia Soul. You can't judge me, Kia Soul. You don't even know me!

Data had whispered and I had a choice in that moment to listen to it or ignore it.

By ignoring it, I'd gain a few pounds, feel bad about myself, wear Spanx on stage at speaking events (for my posture, of course, not my belly), and then eventually come up with some impossible health goal. Cue black beans and perfectionism!

You have the same choice to listen to data, too. A hundred times a day, it is trying to tell you something. We assume it is trying to ruin our fun; we believe that data is the ultimate killjoy.

I remember the first time I saw a restaurant menu that had the calories listed on it. I was in New York City with a large group of people attending a conference. We opened the menus with such vigor and excitement. We were on a pseudo vacation. We were going to eat bold food in a bold city!

A hush immediately fell over our group when we saw the calories next to each entrée. We all changed our orders. Monstrous cheeseburgers, the kind they just jam a knife directly into the top of because you'll need it to slay that beast, became salads. Sad salads, with thin pale strips of grilled chicken, dressing on the side.

What's your weakest dressing? Not Hidden Valley. What are they hiding? I bet it's calories. Please give me your thinnest vinaigrette, one step up from light brown water, please.

Data doomed us in that moment.

It wasn't the restaurant's fault. They didn't want to list the calories; they were forced by law to put them on there. Nothing kills your appetizer and dessert sales like telling someone the obvious—bacon-jalapeño-loaded cheese fries are not healthy. Any dessert that has the word "molten" in it is probably not fat free.

Data, you're the worst.

Why do you hate us so?

Only, what if it doesn't?

What if we've been looking at data the wrong way all these years?

What if data wasn't trying to ruin your day; it was trying to save your life?

What if gathering even a little data could make a huge difference in your ability to knock out your goals?

What if data was one of the best ways to kill perfectionism?

Data Hates Denial

When you ignore data, you embrace denial.

The cheeseburger had the same amount of calories whether I knew about them or not. Data didn't add calories to the meal; it just told me what they were. It gave me everything I needed to make an educated decision in that moment. It tried to help me and my current collection of pants.

I might have been frustrated—a cheeseburger is better than a salad; don't even bother arguing otherwise—but my anger was misguided.

We get mad because we focus on the wrong part of the phrase "Ignorance is bliss." We think data is trying to ruin our bliss and miss that it's actually trying to prevent us from being ignorant.

Denial makes you ignorant.

The most troubling aspect of denial is that the only people we can't recognize it in are ourselves. Spotting denial in other people is incredibly easy and often pretty satisfying. Right now, it's not difficult for you to call to mind a friend who is deep in the throes of denial. They are driving a car they cannot afford. They are on their fiftieth diet but continually enjoying "cheat days." They desperately want a new job but have not applied for any in six months. They are dating an idiot whom they hope marriage will miraculously fix. (If marriage doesn't fix things, try having a baby together. That usually does the trick.)

Denial is neon in others and invisible in you.

Why did we discuss cutting our goals in half at the beginning of this book? Because perfectionism was using denial against us. Perfectionism wanted us to deny reality and chase goals so large we'd be crippled before we even started. The athlete who didn't swim, run, or bike much but wanted to do a 70-mile triathlon was living in denial.

Your emotions cloud your judgment. They form a perfect smoke screen for denial, making your path in life feel murky and confusing. In the fog of feelings, it's hard to see what's really happening.

Data doesn't lie, though. It is not swayed by emotion. It is not subject to the drunken whims of feelings.

Disaster is always the final destination of denial.

No one ever says, "I just kept buying cat after cat after cat, until one day I owned two hundred and things eventually worked themselves out. The cats formed a tribunal and elected a governess who managed the feline community's day-to-day activities."

No one ever says, "The more I surfed online during work, the higher my star rose in the company."

No one ever says, "The secret of my health success? Lard and Lucky Strikes."

There's no denying where denial leads if we ignore data. The good news, dare I say the great news, is this:

Data kills denial, which prevents disaster.

But only if you'll listen to it.

Why You Probably Don't Need an 80-Year-Old Scotch

I once asked a food industry expert if he'd ever seen a refusal to deal with data and the problem of perfectionism hurt a restaurant. He laughed and told me a story about a business that was sprinting toward failure.

"I worked with a chef who had a twenty-two-dollar meal he was serving. He was using a thirteen-dollar piece of meat and a six-dollar sauce to make it. He had nineteen dollars in that meal before he turned on the lights, paid for his lease, purchased his equipment, or hired people to serve the food. The sauce was six dollars! Why? Because he was making it with an eighty-year-old Scotch."

Most people don't have palates that can distinguish minute gradations of quality in Scotch. Sure, you might be able to tell if a Scotch came from a plastic bottle on the bottom shelf of a Panama City Beach gas station or if it came out of a hand-carved mahogany box from a safe behind the counter, but you're not picking up notes of pencil shavings and particular foggy moors in Edinburgh. And that's Scotch that hasn't been lit on fire as part of a sauce.

There's a chance that if the chef used a 40-year-old Scotch instead of the 80-year-old Scotch, very few people would rebel. Most patrons would not say, "Hold on a second, is this thing only four decades old? I demand sauces made with ingredients from before we walked on the moon! What is this swill?!"

But chefs are artists and artists are prone to perfectionism. I promise that chef wanted the "perfect Scotch" for that recipe. In the same way that perfectionism demanded we chase goals bigger than we could really accomplish, perfectionism told this chef only the most expensive Scotch would do. Cheaper Scotches don't count.

Given the choice of go out of business or changing the Scotch, even the cockiest chef would get a cheaper bottle.

If the chef wanted to lower his fourth-quarter expenses, if that was his goal, the Scotch decision would become easy.

That's the whole point of data—it makes things easy.

It is not emotional. It's just data.

In fact, by the end of this book, as you sprint toward your goal, that will be a phrase you find yourself saying out loud: "It's just data."

Data will save you in career decisions as well.

Data told Steve Butler that he needed to take some free classes online.

After losing his job, he had to take the next job he could get. Not the best job, because he had a lot of commitments as a married father of two, but the next job. He applied for several positions and got a good-enough job.

The good-enough job covered some of his bills, but data told him it wasn't going to cover every bill. He could have felt shame about that, he could have beat himself up, but instead he listened to the data. In addition to his full-time job, he got a part-time job cleaning a dental office on the weekends.

"I hated to spend four hours on Saturday morning cleaning the dentist office. I'd come home and my neighbor would be in his front yard throwing the football with his son and I'd be overwhelmed at all the moments I missed with my own son that Saturday. But I knew I had to do both jobs."

He wasn't failing as a father, he was going through some short-term pain for the long-term future of his family. He was knocking out a big goal.

Most people get used to situations and get stuck. They ignore the data until disaster forces them to make a hurried, ill-prepared life change. Not Steve. He knew that his good-enough job wasn't going to be his forever job. So he invested in an intensive career-profiling exercise. The results suggested that he might be well suited for the computer industry. He'd never considered that, but the more he studied the data the more that made sense.

As with any life change, perfectionism got mouthy. Steve worried that if he changed careers, if he explored the computer industry, he would be wasting his college degree. That's a valid concern. Everyone wants to make sure that their college degree was worth it, but in this case, data came to the rescue.

Steve was forty-eight and graduated when he was twenty-two. He finished college at a time when four years of education cost about $50,000. That means he paid $50,000 for a degree that he used successfully for twenty-six years. He got almost three decades of service out of his degree, at only $5.20 per day. What a deal! Data showed him that the fear of "wasting your college degree" was foolish if you've enjoyed it for twenty-six years already.

Instead of quitting his job in an emotional "just go for it, follow your heart moment," Steve continued to look at the data. Data always encourages us to stack the deck in our favor.

He decided to take some free classes online so that he could explore what part of the computer industry he was best suited for. Was he a systems analyst guy? Was he a programmer? Was he a network person? Without the data that taking the classes would reveal, he'd be flying blind.

But taking classes online is easier said than done, right?

We're all too busy.

People tell me this constantly. I have some goals, things I want to do, but I don't have time.

To that pushback, I'd simply say, "What is the data telling you?"

When Steve looked at his week, he didn't just see days and hours, he saw data. Cleaning the dentist office on the weekends and playing with his kids didn't allow much time on Saturday and Sunday. Connecting with his wife and with friends, filled a lot of his evenings. He couldn't take the classes via audiobook while he drove to work, so his commute was unusable. The data told him that the only free time he had was during his lunch break on the weekdays.

So every day during lunch, he took his iPad to the car and took the free classes. Day by day, class by class, he finished. He wanted to take an intensive, all-day six-week class that cost $20,000. That would have been the perfect approach, but the data told him he couldn't afford to miss six weeks of work and he couldn't pay $20,000 out of pocket toward something that was only a curiosity at this point. That would have been like pouring an 80-year-old bottle of Scotch on a piece of steak. Data helped him see that his inability to take the shorter route wasn't failure, it was wisdom.

That's one of the great things about data.

It's a shame killer. At any point during his hustle, Steve could have felt bad about himself:

At my age, I should have a better job.

If I was a better dad, I wouldn't have to work on weekends.

It would all be perfect if I could take faster classes.

It would all be perfect if I didn't have to go at such a slow pace.

Perfectionism marched a parade down Steve's street, but data blew up each float with the truth.

Data told him his average job had a noble purpose—to meet his family's needs.

Data told him working four hours on a Saturday wasn't the whole weekend and he was doing it to support his family, and was not ignoring them.

Data told him taking classes an hour at a time during a lunch break was the only pace he could go at and was therefore ideal.

Data won't allow shame to take root.

Steve is still on the job hunt, but he's got something on his side that most people don't have: data.

You need data. If you really want to stack the deck in your favor, you need math on your side. The first way to make that happen is to measure backward.

Know Where You Came from to Get Where You're Going

Most people look at the finish line when they find themselves in the middle of a goal. This is natural. A lot of our motivational literature teaches this approach. "Don't look back, you're not going that way." "Your past doesn't define your future," we're told. But there's a danger in overfocusing on the finish line.

When you do, you lose the power of seeing how far you've come.

It's a lot more encouraging to look at where you've come from than where you're headed when in the middle of a goal. That changes when you're close to the finish line. Once you're 80 or 85 percent of the way done, it's a different story. Seeing the final stretch can propel you, but when you're firmly in the middle of a goal, the finish line feels too far away to provide a boost of any kind.

Think about it this way: If your goal is to get to 100 percent and you're only at 40, you've failed. That's an F right now, and perfectionism would love to remind you of that. You've still got 60 percent to go. You're not even halfway yet. Ugh.

What if instead you looked at the zero of the starting line and could admit you're not there anymore. The reality is that 40 percent is monstrous progress when compared to zero, but miniscule when compared to 100. When you look back, you can barely see where you were. You've come a long way.

Has the progress changed? Not really, the number is the same, but your interpretation of it is very different. Dan Sullivan, a well-known marketing expert, says that entrepreneurs often struggle with this. They don't just overfocus on the finish line; they move their horizon, never actually hitting their goal because they keep changing the definition of success.

Sometimes, to make it through the middle, we have to be very deliberate about our perception.

My friend Chad Nikazy taught me a powerful lesson about perception. He's a triathlete and once volunteered to guide a blind participant through a race. The swim and bike portions were amazing to read about, but it was the running that surprised me the most.

During the race, Jeremy, the blind athlete, told Chad, "Don't tell me when we're on hills, okay? I can't see them, so I don't feel them. They don't bother me."

The only way he knew he was on a hill was if Chad told him. He found the race easier if he controlled his perception of it.

Is there a more convicting idea about the company you keep? Right now, isn't it easy to think of people who tell you about each and every hill in your life? They're not like Chad, hiding the hills from you. They're doing just the opposite. But our community isn't the issue here.

Trying to finish any goal is like running uphill. At the top is the finish line and in the middle it feels so far away. If you stare up the hill, it's easy to get discouraged. You'll never reach that moment. Fitting into that old dress feels impossible. An empty, clean garage you can park in seems unreachable. Seeing your finished book on a real shelf in a real bookstore feels unrealistic. The distance is simply too much.

But look at zero. Look at the starting line. Look at the bottom of the hill. Do you see how far you've come? Do you see how much progress you've made? Do you see what you've done already?

You will, but only if you measure it.

Twenty-three Ways to Measure Your Goal

We instinctively know we should measure our goals, but most of us don't. Millions of people wearing Fitbits can tell you the number of fictional floors they've climbed or that they just received the badge for walking the equivalent of the entire continent of South America. If you were to ask them how they're measuring their life goals, though, you would be met with a blank stare.

It sounds difficult or complicated or scientific, but if you've made it this far in the book, you've already got at least one measurement. You've read 75 percent. You're already rare and you've already got a measurement of pages. If you've been doing some or all of the actions, you've already got a list of those piling up, too.

What if you want to measure something that's more specific to your goal? What if you want to use data to tear down the phantom of perfectionism that ruins most of your goals?

Here are twenty-three things you can keep track of:

1. Time invested

How many hours during the next 30 days will you invest in your goal? If you spend 15 minutes a day for 30 days, that adds up to 7.5 hours. That might not seem like a lot, but when was the last time you took almost a whole workday to work on something you care about?

2. Money earned

If you've got a business goal, it's easy to measure revenue you've generated during the thirty days.

3. Products sold

Most forms of measurement can be broken down into multiple bits of information. If you're selling a product, it's easy to measure both the money earned and the number of units you sold.

4. Pounds lost

Is there an easier form of measurement than a scale when you're trying to lose weight?

5. Inches

This might be slightly more difficult than tracking your pounds, but knowing how many inches you dropped can also be helpful.

6. Garbage bags full of stuff

A friend of mine who wanted to declutter her house counted the individual items she got rid of but also the number of garbage bags of stuff she donated.

7. Books sold

You never know you own too many books until you have to move and realize a book is just a brick with words. Lots of people who focus on decluttering count the number of books they sell back to the used-book store in their town.

8. Pages or words written

Speaking of books, if you want to write one, counting pages written can be a great thing to measure.

9. Miles run

I'll do about a thousand miles this year. How do I know? Because the Nike app tracks it all for me. I'm almost at Purple Level, a completely useless but oddly satisfying digital reward. I'm already judging those lazy Blue Level losers I left in my dust.

10. Steps

There are lots of great devices on the market right now that will give you this information from the convenience of your own wrist.

11. E-mail subscribers

If you're building any sort of online business, the number of people you have on your e-mail list will be critical.

12. Followers on a social media platform

Save for Snapchat, every social media platform makes it incredibly easy to instantly know how many followers you have.

13. Meals made

Increasing your exercise while ignoring what you eat is stupid. One of the keys to healthy living is meal planning. You could count the number of meals you made each week at home instead of going out.

14. Money saved

You know that number in your savings account? That's a form of measurement.

15. Debt paid off

The thinness of your credit card statement is a form of measurement. If it's being mailed to you with a binder clip and the mailman is out of breath when he delivers it, see if you can work your way down to a single staple.

16. Dates with a spouse

Jenny and I go out five times a week and spend a lot of time holding hands while watching the sunset from two different claw-footed bathtubs in a field. Not really, I just feel a bunch of shame whenever someone tells me how perfect he is at dating his spouse. Time spent with your spouse is time well invested. Keeping track of the number of dates you go on can be great.

17. Prospects contacted

Maybe your business isn't ready to receive sales yet or you're still in the early stages of development. No problem, just keep track of the number of prospects you contacted.

18. Hours slept

Sleep is becoming a hot topic as more people realize it's a key to high performance. (How did this take us so long to realize?) Track it simply with an alarm clock or get more specific with a wearable device.

19. Thank-you notes mailed

Maybe you're working on gratefulness. How many thank-you cards did you send out this month?

20. New contacts

We hate the word "networking," but maybe part of your goal is to expand your network, not just your social media reach. How many people did you meet this month?

21. Bad food avoided

I think it can be equally interesting to track what you didn't do. If you skipped three pieces of pizza and four sodas, write that down. You'll have fun adding up all the calories you didn't eat this month in one imaginary pile, like a Jabba the Hutt made of junk food. *Spaceballs* reference.

22. Books read

This is a fairly common goal and one that's ridiculously easy to keep track of. How many books did you read this month?

23. Hours of TV watched

Maybe your goal is to cut back on TV. This one is simple, especially if your preferred method of watching is Netflix which you can easily measure.

Those are just twenty-three examples and more than likely your unique goal has some unique forms of progress you can measure.

All I want you to do is pick one to three things you'll measure. Why so few? Because when it goes well, and it will, you'll want to measure more. I won't even need to encourage you. You'll just do it on your own. It's fun to see progress and you'll intuitively understand that if three points of progress are enjoyable to watch, maybe five would be even better.

That's part of the reason that fantasy football is such a sticky activity. You get to track so many different points of progress. And it's also proof that you can measure things. If you've ever played fantasy football, I promise you can do this, too.

Don't overdo it. Perfectionism would have you measure thirty different things, weighing out the grams of vegetables on a scale to make sure you were getting exactly the right amount of potassium. Pump the brakes. Choose one to three points of data. That's it.

The Past Is Trying to Teach You

Data flows in two directions, forward and backward. The list of items we just discussed are forward points of data. You'll keep track of them going forward. Backward data is just as important, though, and is a collection of information from how things went in the past.

The past can be highly educational, but I usually don't like to learn from it.

For instance, it took me fifty-eight long TSA lines before I invested seven minutes into getting TSA Pre so I could speed through security at the airport.

Why don't we learn from the past? Perfectionism tells us this is simply one more form of cheating. We don't need the past! That's another crutch. Remember, perfectionism is aggressively opposed to anything that makes our goal easier, and learning from the past certainly does that.

It's time to plumb your past to figure out if history is teaching you anything. Is something you've already done before trying to inform your next time? This is another one of those "don't get lost in the list" moments. If you're prone to drifting and getting tangled in exercises, just answer the first three and move on. Don't go all perfect on me.

Let's ask a few questions:

1. What happened last time you attempted a goal like the one you're planning?

    Be honest here. You don't need to shine up the results to impress anyone; no one else will be reading your notes. And pick something fairly recent because we tend to misremember things the further we get from them. It doesn't have to be something you finished, just something you attempted.

2. If you haven't done this goal before, what happened with a similar goal?

    Getting on a budget might feel very different from the time you knocked out a diet, but they're both restrictive goals. (You're eating less and spending less.) There are similarities you can learn from here.

3. Who was involved last time?

I hate words like "solopreneur" because they perpetuate the idea that you're going to knock out a goal by yourself. You won't. No one is truly a solopreneur. You don't deliver your own mail. No matter your goal, there are going to be other people involved and affected.

4. How long did it take?

Was it a month? A week? Six months? Knowing this will help you accurately measure the progress of your new goal.

5. How much money do you need to finish it?

Is there a budget for your goal? Money usually isn't the first thing you need to invest; time is, but it probably will become a factor eventually. How much did it cost you to work on a goal last time? Did you go over budget? Was it hard keeping track of the expenses? Did the cost of anything surprise you?

6. Was there a deadline? (The project has to launch by _____)

A deadline can be one of the greatest levers to finishing. Did you use one last time? Did it help or create unnecessary pressure?

7. Were there consequences if you didn't finish it?

Consequences cause change. Without them, we lose focus. The last time you tried something, were the consequences of not finishing clear? What were they? Did they motivate you?

8. If you finished, did you get a reward?

If you're motivated by a prize, did you get one? If you didn't finish, was it because you had the wrong prize? Maybe no prize at all? What sort of reward was triggered by the completion of this goal?

9. If you didn't finish, which part tripped you up?

Traveling makes healthy eating difficult for me. Traveling and burritos, actually. The older I get, the more I realize that failure is educational. When I slip, it's important that I ask a few questions or I am going to slip again.

10. If you could do it differently this time, what would you change?

If you tried the same goal again, how would you approach it from a different angle?

The goal of asking all these questions and gathering as much information as possible is to give you the greatest shot at success.

The questions above aren't magical and they're not the end. If anything, they're just the beginning of the interview you should do with the things you want to finish. The better your questions, the better your data, the better your odds at being successful. Please make sure you read the word "better" in that last sentence and not "perfect."

I know this is a lot of work, and I assure you I am doing my best to distract you with humor and pop culture references. These exercises are as awkward as when Jimmy Kimmel asked James Corden how much he disliked his "Carpool Karaoke" segment with Britney Spears. Relevant!

The work is worth it, especially if you have a goal you really care about. Keep in mind that you might realize along the way that you need a new goal. The exercises we're doing are nothing in comparison with the real work of making it through the middle of a project. All I'm asking you to create is a list of actions. If you don't want to do that, how do you think you'll feel when you actually have to do the actions? Writing down "Make cold calls to potential clients" is infinitely easier than actually doing it when the time rolls around.

Changing your goal here is not failure. It's success! I'd much rather you refine your goal or pick a better one than have you limp through a process that's difficult, with a goal that doesn't matter to you.

When a Plane Is More Than a Plane

Reviewing your past is one of the best ways to understand who you really are and how you'll work best on a goal. Keep in mind that perfectionism can't stand self-awareness. If you're self-aware, you're more likely to know and accept your limitations, which means you won't fall for the promise of a perfect performance. Self-awareness might also make you want to fly more often.

I have three friends who claim they are able to finish more projects when they are on planes than any other time. I've heard this type of thing from people of all walks of life and professions.

Most people will stop right there, never questioning what that really means, but great finishers explore the big idea behind the small one. What is it about the plane that makes you so productive? It's not the air quality, because you are breathing in every type of germ all at once. Whenever I see families all traveling with face masks on, I think, "What do you know that I don't?"

It's not bringing your pillow on the flight, which is the grossest thing currently happening in air travel. I've never slept in my own bed and thought, "You know what would make this better? If my personal pillow had rubbed against a seat on an airplane."

It's not the beverage service. There's nothing sadder than watching an executive in coach who is flying to Baltimore to negotiate a $10-million-dollar real estate deal ask for the "whole can of ginger ale." I know I can handle it. Please leave it with me.

It's not the spacious seats or the 7 degrees of recline or the elbow power struggle that every shared armrest represents. So then why are people productive on planes?

There are several possibilities:

1. You can only bring a limited amount of work.

     At your office on the ground you can work on everything all at once. You are surrounded by filing cabinets, desks, and drawers packed with other projects. The limited amount of carry-on space and microscopic nature of the pull-down tray eliminates distractions. You might want to bring the flooring plans for the new building and the project scope and your dry erase board and your laptop, but you don't have the room. In addition to eliminating distractions, airplanes also force you to plan and pack deliberately. The projects you work on aren't accidental or random.

2. The white noise helps you focus.

Planes are loud. I'm not sure if you knew that. Thrusting tons of metal into the sky and battling gravity is apparently a difficult feat to pull off quietly. For many people, this blanket of white noise helps them get into the zone. It's so loud it becomes quiet. (That might be the most kung fu thing I say in this entire book.)

3. The Internet connection is too weak to get distracted.

I love and hate the Internet. I love it because it offers me the opportunity to do anything. I hate it because it offers me the opportunity to do everything. For a lot of travelers, the spotty Internet connection offers the forced isolation from digital distractions they might have a hard time creating naturally on earth. You also can't get texts on airplanes, which is why when you land you'll often hear people groan as waves of messages hit their phones all at once now that there's a signal. *Game of Thrones* author George R. R. Martin creates his own disconnected setup by writing his books on a DOS-based word processor from the 1980s.

4. There's a well-defined deadline.

A flight is a finite, tiny thing. There is a definite conclusion. There's actually a set of conclusions. You have a window to work before they board in the terminal. Then you have a few minutes while they are loading the plane. You then have to put up your laptop and wait until you hit ten thousand feet to pull it back out. There's even an announcement that it's time to put away your laptop. For most people, this is the first time since grade school they've had such structure. Comedian Demetri Martin used this deadline to make the transition between amateur comedian and professional. "When I started, it was fun because they [jokes] would just come to me and I'd write them down in my notebook when they came. But when it became a job, I realized I couldn't wait around anymore. Planes are good because I'll say, "OK, I'll write 100 jokes between here and NYC/LA. No matter if they're good."

5. Nobody knows you.

A plane might be a great place for you to work because you're anonymous. Unless you're me, and autographed all the copies of your picture in *Southwest* magazine because you want the stranger in the middle seat to know you're doing stuff with your life. Save for the flight attendant or a chatty seatmate who can be quieted down by making a showy presentation of putting on your headphones, you won't be bothered on a plane. No one is coming into your office and saying the biggest lie in the history of the English language: "You got a minute?" That minute is never sixty seconds long.

By looking at a situation for a few minutes, you can get some awareness. The next step is to turn that awareness into action.

If you realize you do great work on airplanes, you might not be able to take a thousand flights a year to ensure you're productive. But you can take the principles and apply them to other parts of your life.

If, for instance, the limited amount of work helps you focus, leave the office with only one file. If the spotty Internet connection helps you be present, turn your phone off during the next coffee you have with a friend.

If you don't learn what makes you work best and repeat it, you'll never get better.

Think about a time when you accomplished something. What were you doing? What elements of that moment helped the most? Where were you? What music were you listening to? What did you do before? What did you do after?

What works for me won't work for you. The uniqueness of my goal, intricacy of my personality, and jump-out-of-the-gym vertical leap makes us pretty different. I can't work at home, for instance. It makes me really depressed. I know our goal as a country is to work from home in our pajamas, but I find trying to work in sweatpants to be one of the saddest things ever. I'm not saying I have to wear uncomfortable burlap pants or a tuxedo with tails, but I have to leave the house to get anything done.

It took me two years to learn that ridiculously simple idea. I spent fifteen years commuting to an office. I knew that rhythm. I was good with that pace. Then I started my own company and floundered for two years at home, frustrating my wife, over-talking to our UPS guy out of desperation for community, and not knowing why.

Perfectionism told me that every other entrepreneur loved to work at home. I was the only one having a hard time with it. What was wrong with me?

If I had stopped for ten minutes and asked, "How do I work best?" I would have quickly realized that I needed a commute. It doesn't have to be a soul-crushing L.A. version, but I need at least a few minutes in the car to shake off the slumber and get in the work zone. I had fifteen years of evidence that tried to tell me that. Don't ignore how you work best as you figure out how to finish.

Gilana Telles did a little self-evaluation the first time she went through the 30 Days of Hustle and realized she performs well with a complex system of her own personal creation. "I com-pleted sixty-two important tasks that I otherwise would have pushed back and left for the last minute. I developed a chart to track my goals by week. I created a color-coded calendar system!"

What works for her would give me a panic attack. Just the phrases "color-coded calendar system" and "sixty-two import-ant tasks" make me feel a little bit sweaty. For Gilana it worked, but only because she paid attention to her strengths and then turned them into actions.

Three Ways to Respond to the Progress

You've looked at forward data. You've studied backward data, too, but what if the numbers aren't where you'd like them to be? This is what I call a "perfectionism pause" moment. Perfectionism loves to stop you midway through a goal. Why do 92 percent of resolutions fail? Because after doing something like gathering data, all those goal setters thought they were done. But data you collect and don't use is useless.

What if you collected data and the results aren't what you were hoping for? That's why a lot of people quit. They give in to disappointment and unmet expectations.

If you're unhappy with your progress, you have three different dials you can adjust.

1. The goal
2. The timeline
3. The actions

The goal is your finish line, what you set out to accomplish when you started this project. For Jason, the dieter who wanted to lose weight because an elderly relative made a crack about him, the goal was the forty pounds. If you find out you're nowhere near hitting your goal, you might need to turn that dial down. Perhaps the problem was that Jason wanted to lose an unreasonable forty pounds and was better off shooting for twenty. We have already discussed in length the value of cutting your goal in half.

The second dial Jason, and you, have access to is the timeline. Instead of giving himself eight weeks to see progress, he could increase that to sixteen weeks. If his goal was stretched out over time, he could greatly increase his chance of seeing the progress he wanted. We've covered that one already, too.

The third dial represents the actions you're taking to get to the finish line. When faced with disappointing results, Jason had the option to turn that dial. He could increase his actions. In addition to working with a personal trainer, he could hire a dietitian to come up with an eating plan. He could swear off caloric rich beer and wine. He could increase the number of days he was exercising each month.

It's good to note that in work-related finish projects, you sometimes don't have access to those first two dials. When you review the results and realize you're not going to hit your goal, you might not have the freedom to tell your boss, "I'm going to decrease the sales I promised to get and double my timeline! I know we need to launch that project for the client in time for the opening of their new hospital wing, but I've been messing around some with the timeline dial, so it's not going to happen."

In situations like that, all of your focus and energy need to be placed on the actions dial. You'll have to dramatically increase your actions if you have a finish line you must cross. Just make sure that an increase in action doesn't come with an increase in perfection.

In personal projects it's easier to deal with all three dials because you're the one in charge.

Instead of beating yourself up, instead of misremembering how easy it was in the past, instead of quitting, look at the three dials. Do you need to tweak your goal, your timeline, or your actions?

Don't wait until the squirrels come home.

I am not naturally good at data, and most of the time I hate it.

But do you know what I hate even more? Perfection. I hate feeling lost because I don't know which is the best way to go. I hate living in denial. And more than anything, I hate disaster.

When we lived in Alpharetta, Georgia, a small bit of rot developed on the corner of our roof. I'd never owned a home before, so I didn't really know what to do with that data. "Huh, look at that, a hole from our attic directly to the outside world. Neat."

Every time I mowed the backyard I would look up and see it getting larger. For months, I watched the progress as the corner of our house disintegrated. I had the data. There was a six-inch hole, but I didn't do anything with it. I denied it would be a problem because I was afraid that if I really investigated it, we couldn't afford to fix it.

Fortunately, the hole fixed itself. Our house was like Wolverine and had self-healing properties. We bought that from Nationwide. Turns out they were on our side.

Actually, what happened first was the ants. One day, we didn't have any ants. The next day, there were a hundred thousand living in the corner of our great room. Jenny was upset but the spiders sure weren't. They immediately set up webs in the corner twenty feet above our couch. Now, in addition to the pulsating-ceiling ant colony, we had webs full of dead bodies. It started to look like an insect Burning Man up there, with different species of bugs showing up to set up camp around the ant buffet.

I might have ignored the ants forever—denial is a powerful thing—but the squirrels were difficult to write off. A squirrel family decided to move into the attic. You'll never sleep more peacefully than when you can hear a tree rat scurrying around right above your head in the attic, one with never-ending fangs. Did you know that? The reason squirrels chew on metal on your roof is that their teeth never stop growing. That's not terrifying at all.

What was a hundred-dollar hole turned into thousands of dollars of repair, especially after I tried to catch the squirrels and had a friend step through our bedroom ceiling. I pointed out to Jenny the convenience of being able to see what's in our attic without evening leaving our bed, but she didn't view the hole that way. She's closed-minded like that.

Don't wait until the squirrels move in to listen to data.

Data kills denial, which prevents disaster.

Perfection will tell you that your data must be complicated. If you dare to gather some, it will have you tracking every ounce of water, second of time, and vowels used in the book you're writing.

Don't.

Our goal in this chapter is to get one to three points we can use. For what? To finish, which is what we're about to do.

Actions:

1. Write down one to three things you can track concerning your goal.
2. Review a goal from the past to see if you can learn anything.
3. Find your airplane. What's the way you work best?
4. If you're already in the middle of a goal, decide if you need to adjust your goal, timeline, or actions.

CHAPTER 8

The Day Before Done

I've never seen someone quit at mile 25 of a marathon.

I've never seen someone say, "You know what? I'm almost done. I can see the finish line, but I don't like free bananas. It's time to call it a day."

I've never seen a runner who is afraid to finish.

On the contrary, I've seen bloodied, beaten, exhausted athletes go faster the last mile. I've seen triathletes crawl across the finish line, their bodies wrecked but their will intact.

That was the moment they strived for, that was the moment they spent all those months training for. That was the most important moment of all.

So then why do starters have such a hard time with the day before done?

Why did Meredith Bray spend six years in undergrad, change majors two times, attend six different schools, only to fail her last final on purpose, ensuring she wouldn't graduate? Why did she refuse to finish for twenty-three more years, requiring open-heart surgery to motivate her to finally graduate?

Why did an artist friend spend six to eight hours creating an art piece, only to shred it before she completed it? Better question, why did she do this a hundred different times, to works of art she now sells for $275?

Because the day before done is terrifying.

One Last Shot

In the 1980s, 92 percent of all romantic comedies involved someone sprinting through an airport. Back then there wasn't much security. You could show up at any airport and essentially say, "I'm going to the terminal to look at airplanes." One tired security guard, who didn't have access to an X-ray machine and thus was unable to really know whether you had any batarangs about your person, would wave you through. No questions, no pat-downs, no need to explain why you require four ounces of hair pomade for a three-day trip.

And if it happened that your one true love was about to get on a plane and get out of your life, you were allowed to make a mad dash through the airport.

You might not normally be a "bump strangers or jump small dogs that are clearly not really service animals" kind of person, but on that day you were willing to be because it was your last shot at happiness. Your entire relationship came down to that moment, and there was nothing you wouldn't do to save it. You were desperate.

That's how perfection feels about the day before done.

You fought through the day after perfect. You cut your goal in half. You killed your cuckoos. You made sure your goal is fun. You are inches away from finished and perfectionism knows it.

It only has one last chance to wreck the whole thing, one last opportunity to topple the entire goal.

And unfortunately, most people never see it coming.

We don't talk about it. We know the middle is a grind. We understand collectively that there will be doldrums in the center of any endeavor. That's when the going gets tough.

But have you ever heard anyone say, "The worst part of my goal was when the finish line was in sight?" Of course not. We believe the finish line is a magnet pulling us toward it, as if, perhaps, momentum will carry us across on its own volition. We're half right; it is a magnet, but usually it's the polar opposite, pushing against you, not pulling with you.

Into that space, perfection gets louder. Like a villain you only winged and refused to disarm John Wick–style, it rises back up for one more barrage of fear.

And these last three fears are doozies.

The Three Final Fears of Perfection

It's not uncommon to experience the fear of success as you get closer to finishing. That's fairly normal and something we discussed at length when we reviewed cuckoos that needed immediate elimination. But in addition to that garden-variety concern, there are three different fears associated with the finish line. You will hear one or perhaps all of these the closer you get to done.

1. The fear of what happens next

Sometimes you're not afraid of the finish; you're afraid of what happens after the finish. It's one thing to complete your book. It's another thing to have that book open to feedback from strangers on Amazon. John Steinbeck described this perfectly with his character Henri in *Cannery Row*. (It's weird that he predicted Amazon a hundred years earlier than it came out, but such was the power of Steinbeck.) Henri was a master shipbuilder but he never finished, despite working for years. At the last minute, just as he approached completion, he'd tear up the boat and start again. Most of his friends thought he was crazy, but one understood what was happening. "Henri loves boats but he's afraid of the ocean. . . . He likes boats. . . . But suppose he finishes his boat. Once it's finished people will say, 'Why don't you put it in the water?' Then if he puts it in the water, he'll have to go out in it, and he hates the water. So you see, he never finishes the boat—so he doesn't ever have to launch it."

Henri was afraid of the water. What are you afraid of? Is it criticism? Strangers can't critique your thing if it's never done. It's easier to hide your idea in a box under your bed than it is to share it with the world.

Be honest, are there a dozen half-finished boats attached to your dock right now? Do you keep almost launching? In these situations, we think if we don't finish we'll be spared some hardship, but that's not true.

Talent you don't claim turns into bitterness eventually. When asked what he would have done if he never became a writer, Stephen King said, "I probably would have died of alcoholism around age 50. And I'm not sure my marriage would have lasted. I think people are extremely hard to live with when they have a talent they aren't able to use."

Boats were built for water. You'll figure out what's next when you get there. Don't worry about it now.

2. The fear that it won't be perfect

I read 7.9 of the 8 Harry Potter books. Not sure what that means? You must be a normal person. I bet that's nice. I didn't want the series to end and was afraid that the ending wouldn't be amazing. So I got right up to the line, read thousands of pages, and then I quit. The book is still on my shelf, shaming me.

I'm not the only one who does that, though. On Facebook, Matt Bunk told me, "I watched every season of *Breaking Bad* and then stopped 4 episodes from the end. I just didn't want it to end badly, so I just stopped watching."

This happens with books and movies and goals because perfectionism throws one last pitch at you. As you round the last corner, it gets louder. "Oh, almost done. How exciting! I hope it's everything you want it to be. Wouldn't that be terrible if it wasn't? Can you imagine? That would be a letdown. I'm sure it will be fine, though. It will be euphoric. I just know it will."

Hold on, you think. What if perfectionism is right? What if it's not amazing?

The previously mentioned artist who was prone to shred her work, struggled with this same fear. Why did she destroy her art? Because "it wasn't perfect." On the verge of completion, that realization would hit her and she'd tear up something she'd spent hours creating.

What if for years you've dreamed about seeing your book on a shelf in a store, and when you do, it's not the best feeling in the world? What if the scale hits the number you've been dieting toward and the crust of the earth doesn't shatter in raucous response? What if you make a million dollars and it doesn't complete you Jerry Maguire–style?

Those are all legitimate questions, and I'm going to answer them the same way I've been answering those kinds of questions in the entire book.

It won't be perfect. It won't. Not because you did something wrong but because life doesn't work that way.

Life is always a little different than we expected. The colors aren't the same as we saw them in our head. The moment unfolds with a different rhythm than we predicted. The familiar emotions we banked on are different.

I thought that finishing a book would be my moment. In my head I imagined writing "The End" and then walking away from that final page with a smile deeper than I'd ever known. That's not how it has ever happened. I never remember the moment I finish. Do you know what I remember? The moment I get copies of the book in the mail. When I got *Do Over*, McRae, my youngest daughter, and I were the only ones home. I was refreshing the UPS tracking information like a maniac. I couldn't wait to crack open the box.

You can't have perfect, but what you get is even better. You get a surprise. You get something you didn't see coming. Because that's the truth. No one sees it coming. Not even Burt Reynolds.

When he made the movie *Smokey and the Bandit,* there wasn't a script. They ad-libbed the film. It was directed by a stuntman who had never directed a film before. The plot was terrible. Bandit and Cletus must drive from Georgia to Texarkana, Texas, with an illegal shipment of Coors beer. That's not a movie, that's a UPS guy's task list. When asked about the movie, Sally Field said, "I thought it was the end of everything I had worked so hard to achieve."

Contrast that with another movie that had a much better shot at success. It was directed by Jon Favreau, hot off the *Iron Man* franchise. It was produced by Ron Howard of *Apollo 13* fame. It starred Han Solo (Harrison Ford) and James Bond (Daniel Craig).

Two very different movies, with two very different outcomes. *Cowboys & Aliens,* despite having all the earmarks of possible success, bombed. It was an abject failure that made $11 million. What? Like in the first weekend? It only made $11 million? No, that's the total amount of profit the movie made.

What about *Smokey and the Bandit*? That movie made an estimated $300 million and was second the year it came out to a movie called *Star Wars*.

Why should you ignore perfection when it tries to predict something won't be good enough? Because no one knows the outcome until after. Perfectionism sure doesn't. Bon Jovi didn't want to put "Living on a Prayer" on his album. He didn't like the song and thought other people wouldn't either. History is littered with examples like this.

3. The fear of "what now?"

When people say it's lonely at the top, I think they're referring to the unbelievably heavy sense of "what now" that lands on you after you accomplish something. The first fear, what next, is about what happens to the goal you've finished. Dreaming about a business is a lot easier than actually finishing and opening one. "What now" is about finding a new goal entirely. If you've had a single-minded focus on some goal and suddenly it's done, what do you do now? In unhealthy situations, in which the person has turned the goal into their whole identity, this is particularly dangerous. You see this happen to professional athletes and child stars sometimes. From the age of six to thirty, football was your everything. Now, at thirty-one, you're considered old and past your prime. You get cut from the team and suddenly don't know who you are anymore. Then, even worse, you have to do commercials for

Wrangler Jeans. Fortunately for you and me, way back in chapter 5 we prepared for this. You have an entire list of "what now" possibilities. Remember all the next ideas you added to your list? Well, when you finish this goal, you get to pull that back out. I get to work on a podcast, for example. The finish line isn't scary when you realize it's also a starting line for the next thing. It's not the end, it's just a different kind of beginning.

I once stood on the edge of a Central American cliff wondering, "What now?" I'd spent a few weeks during college in Costa Rica learning Spanish for my minor. I went on the trip with thirty other students and was overwhelmed by the reality that the trip was over. I knew that all the cliques that had disappeared when we went on the trip would re-form back at college. I'd never talk to the thirty people I had become friends with. I stood on the edge overlooking the ocean, inventing the emo subculture with my sadness. All around me, people were laughing and having fun, enjoying one of our last nights together, and I was at a private funeral for one.

This was not a moment I dealt with only once. I also feel this sometimes when I speak at events. One day, I spoke to a thousand people in Atlanta. It was an emotional event because it was one I had wanted to speak at for five years. The peak of that moment was incredibly high. After the event, I was supposed to eat dinner with the other speakers, but got the wrong address. Ten minutes after stepping offstage, I found myself standing in a Firehouse Subs parking lot. When I went inside to order a sandwich, five people from the audience were already eating and offered me a seat at their table. They looked at me with a sort of sad, sub-shop pity. "What are you doing here?" they asked. It was an incredibly humbling experience.

I'm not the only one who got crushed by a lack of "what now." In the documentary *Conan O'Brien Can't Stop,* we watch Conan tour the country after getting fired from his show on NBC. The entire film deals with the difficulty of "what now," but none so more than one scene in New York.

Conan has just played a sold-out concert in Radio City Music Hall. There's a massive crowd of people in the streets hoping that he'll come out after the show. One of Conan's employees says, "You're not going out there." Conan, looking stunned, says, "You don't get it. I can't go from this, [performing] to doing what? Reading a Kindle?" With a shrug he heads back outside to bask in some more adulation.

You need an answer to what now. That's a legitimate thing to think through, but again, don't let perfectionism sneak in. It will tell you that you need a perfect answer to what now before you finish. That's nonsense. You don't need to have the next thing figured out before you finish this thing. Finish anyway.

Don't let the fear of what's next steal the joy of finishing what's now. Don't let perfectionism distract you with a fictional second goal when you've got a real one almost done.

If one of those fears doesn't stop you, simple reality will.

It's easier to start a new goal than it is to finish an old one.

It's amazing how attractive all our other desires get the closer we get to completing one. The Sirens who wooed Odysseus had nothing on the distraction of new goals that would shipwreck us in this moment.

It's like watching a thousand movie trailers but never actually finishing a whole film. You'll get a brief burst of excitement but will miss what makes a movie really special if you keep starting a new one over and over again.

Don't lose focus. Don't give in to the new in this moment. Don't quit now. We're so close, and there's someone you need to meet who will make sure you don't.

You Can't Schedule a Crisis but You Can Call a Friend

When you work with people who were stuck and then miraculously had a breakthrough, there are generally two reasons they did.

The first is that they had a life-altering experience. Meredith went back to finish her degree after twenty-three years because she had open-heart surgery and realized how fragile life was.

That's an incredibly powerful form of motivation, but not one you can really plan. I can't have a chapter in this book called "How to Almost Die." A dramatic, near-death experience can't be the solution, despite what happened to Michael Douglas's character in the movie *The Game*. Rich beyond belief and bored,

Douglas is thrust into a life-or-death experience that ends up being an elaborate birthday gift from his brother, Sean Penn.

I'm sure if you're an oil tycoon you have access to things like this, but you're probably not. That leaves us with the second way to make sure you finish. A friend.

Time and again, when I researched what really helped people finally finish, it was a friend who did the trick.

The artist who shredded her work, experienced that first-hand. One day, she mentioned to a friend that she had been destroying the things she made. It wasn't a big intervention moment; she shared it casually, in passing.

The friend's eyes grew wide and he said to her, "No more shredding!" That was the day she quit.

What I love about the story is that the friend didn't give her some eloquent explanation of why she needed to stop. The friend didn't show her a framed photo of other artists and tell a Robin Williams–style story about how they are all quietly telling her "carpe diem." The friend didn't commit to track her progress over the following months and rearrange his entire life. The friend wasn't Morgan Freeman.

I think that's what we want sometimes.

We expect a wise guru to emerge from the shadows of the day and tell us, "Either get busy living or get busy dying." Granted, everything sounds better in Freeman's accent, but the change we need is usually not that elaborate. It's usually not complicated. It's usually not that dramatic.

It's a friend who breaks the habit loop and tells you to stop shredding. It's a friend who tells you the thing you've accepted as normal isn't normal. It's a talk show host who makes fun of you.

That last one probably won't happen to you, but it's what spurred comedian Chris Hardwick to change. One night, Jon Stewart made a comment about Chris on *The Daily Show*. Watching at home, Hardwick was crushed by the jab. He decided that night that he would quit drinking, lose weight, and get his business in order.

Was it easy? Of course it wasn't, but the point is that it started with something small from a fellow comedian and friend.

We need friends during the entire goal, but they are most critical at the finish line.

Go find one, and perhaps even more important, go be one.

Author Josh Shipp spent his childhood bouncing around from foster home to foster home. A lot of teens would have been stuck in that experience, never able to make their way out of that hardship. Josh turned his experience into a mission to help other at-risk kids. One of his favorite sayings is, "Every kid is one caring adult away from being a success story." I love that idea and think it's true of kids. I also believe it's true of adults.

We don't ever age out of needing someone to believe in us.

It's not complicated. It's not difficult. It's not time-consuming. Someone in your circle needs to be told to stop shredding. Unless they're a surfer. And then you need to say the opposite of that, obviously.

Let's Ask One More Question No One Ever Asks

Here's a question you've never asked yourself:

"What am I getting out of not finishing?"

Because you're getting something.

If you've had a goal for a while or one that you've started and routinely quit, there's a reason. You're getting something out of not finishing. There's a piece of cheese somewhere in this maze.

A would-be artist on Facebook told me she knows why she's not finishing. "If I think I might not succeed, I allow everything to keep me from even attempting to achieve my goal."

Do you hear the perfectionism in there? She's afraid she won't succeed, that it won't be perfect.

This is a classic benefit of not finishing. You get to hold on to the illusion that you could finish if you really wanted to. Rather than try to find out you might not be good, you hide in the myth of maybe. That's why my friend Carly won't play her violin for you.

"I've had it for three years, and it's been out of the case twice. I'm terrified of it. If I begin and realize I won't be able to succeed, then the dream of playing the violin someday dies. So it makes so much sense to just leave it in the case forever, right? Nonsense."

Deep down she knows what she's doing because she asked that question. How about you?

What are some common benefits people receive from not finishing? Here are three different things that three people who have a hard time finishing told me:

1. Control over the outcome.

Because if I try, I might fail. If I never try, I at least know the outcome.

2. Praise for being a martyr.

If you are "sacrificing" your goals by focusing on other aspects of life (children, spouse's goals, other life events, for example), you receive accolades from others who are impressed by that "selfless" act.

3. Lowered expectations from other people.

If I try to succeed, then the expectations of perfection will be even higher next time. I'd rather occasionally surprise people with what I can do rather than build up a reputation of success.

If what you gain by not finishing outweighs what you receive by finishing, this book will be useless for you.

I once told my wife that I wish I had better friends, and she said, "No you don't."

I asked her what she meant and she replied, "You're an extrovert with strangers and an introvert with people you know. You use your travel schedule as an excuse to hide from relationships."

You say mean things, Jenny.

She was right. What I gained by avoiding relationships is the safety of thinking I couldn't get hurt by other people if I didn't connect with other people. That problem sounds exactly like the plot of a Lifetime channel movie. "Surrounded by people, alone at home, one man's struggle to accept the risk of relationship."

There were certainly times when I had to pause relationships to focus on a goal, but the longer I held on to what I believed were the benefits of hiding, the longer I'd fail at accomplishing my goal of having friends.

Perfectionism always offers us a distorted, thin version of the world. My friendships were "perfect" in that they didn't hurt, but by never doing the work of being real with friends, my relationships were fake.

What are you getting out of not finishing?

Be honest with yourself. And if you find something, make the reward or fear motivation even bigger.

Imagine a seesaw on a playground. If you've got a massive, admittedly broken, benefit to not finishing on one side, all the hustle on the other side won't matter. The thrill of skiing in my own boots instead of rented torture devices was big enough to overshadow what I got from not finishing my book.

If it wasn't, I would have added skis and maybe even a trip to Colorado to the reward. Identify what you're getting out of not finishing and then tip the scales in your favor, especially as we get closer to the finish line.

Who's Afraid of the Finish Line?

Don't dread the day before done. Fear no finish line. You've worked too hard to give up now.

Does the ocean have some waves? Will there be people who don't get your art? Will the outcome be different from your vision? Yes. I can't lie to you this late in the book. But you'll never know the unbelievable joy of keeping a promise to yourself unless you finish.

That's what we're doing, keeping a commitment to ourselves and knowing we've fulfilled it when we finish.

Actions:

1. Identify which of the final fears of perfectionism you struggle with the most. (If any.)
2. Write down the name of one friend you can reach out to.
3. Answer the question, "What am I getting out of not finishing?"

CONCLUSION

I have a confession.

At least three times a week, I watch YouTube clips of *The Voice*.

And I don't just watch the American version of the show, with Blake Shelton, Pharrell, Gwen Stefani, and Adam Levine. I go down deep rabbit trails that eventually find me enjoying an opera singer audition on *The Voice of Albania*. Hosted by Ledion Lico, of course.

If you've never seen the show, it's a singing contest similar to *American Idol*.

My favorite part is the audition process. Unlike other musical programs, the judges can't see the contestant when they start singing. All four judges are sitting in big chairs that look like the kind of thing a villain in a James Bond movie would own in a volcano lair.

If they like what they hear, the judges can press a big button

187

and spin the chair around to see the person. Sometimes, the person looks exactly like her voice and there's very little surprise. But on the best auditions, the person singing doesn't look at all like her voice.

The judges throw up their hands in complete shock, bang the big button a dozen times, and the audience jumps to its feet for a standing ovation.

This is why people like Susan Boyle and Paul Potts are such fun to watch. Neither one of them looks like they're full of talent. Both of them seem normal and average. You'd walk past them on a street without ever noticing. But when they open their mouths and do the thing they're supposed to do, it's amazing.

For every Paul Potts, though, there are a thousand people who never tried. For every Susan Boyle, there are a thousand shower singers who didn't think they were good enough to even audition.

That's ultimately the worst thing that perfectionism does.

It keeps you home. It traps you on the couch. It makes sure you never try.

It brings you to the last final exam of your six-year college career and then persuades you to fail it on purpose.

I don't know you. We might never meet. You might never get to see that I am really taller in real life. Like basketball tall. Google it.

But I know this, if you've been giving in to perfectionism, it's enough already.

Stop shredding.

Maybe you don't even make it that far. Maybe you can't even bring yourself to drive to the store and buy painting supplies. Maybe your art doesn't even make it to the canvas.

I don't know what obstacle trips you up. I don't know which trap perfectionism uses on you the most. I don't know why you refuse to finish.

I just know there's a moment I want to invite you to: that moment when the unexpected happens, when the judge turns around in his chair and is surprised at what you, little old you, is capable of. I might sound cheesy and not at all cool, but sometimes cool is a form of cowardice to prevent you from admitting the things you deeply care about.

The chair turn is one of my favorite things ever. It's also why I believe in finishing.

Most of us spend most of our lives wondering what if. We imagine. We dream. We hope.

And a week turns into a month turns into a year.

The stage stays empty. The mic stays quiet. The chair won't spin around because no one is singing.

In moments like this, the goal doesn't disappear. We think that perhaps the sands of time will cover it up and we will forget all about it, but we don't. A goal unfulfilled may grow dim, but it never goes dark. A movie character will remind us of the promise, a store window where a book like ours sits or an offhand comment from a friend will stir it all back up.

Goals you refuse to chase don't disappear—they become ghosts that haunt you. Do you know why strangers rage at each other online and are so quick to be angry and offended these days? Because their passion has no other outlet.

When you refuse to deal in joy, you don't quit being emotional; you just funnel all that fury somewhere else. Many a troll was born from the heartache of a goal he dared not finish. Maybe a troll is just someone who lost to perfectionism so many times that he gave up on his own goals and decided to tear down someone else's.

But then, we try. Then we act. Then we fail. Then we try again.

Why do I believe in finishing?

Because I believe in you.

I believe there's more.

Scratch that. I believe there's a lot more.

Why do I believe that?

Because I've seen it a thousand times in a thousand different people working on a thousand different goals.

And if you try even a tenth of the things we talked about in this book, you'll get to see it, too.

Starting is fun, but the future belongs to finishers.

Ready to be one?

ACKNOWLEDGMENTS

I've often thought that this section of the book should be called "Acknowledgments and Apologies." I think that because few things make me as anxious and grumpy as trying to finish a book on deadline. So, let me come right out of the gate and thank my beautiful wife, Jenny, for putting up with me during the longest book process I've ever known. Her patience and contributions made this whole thing possible. Mom and Dad, thanks for believing in me and encouraging me all these years. Jon and Laura Calbert, I couldn't ask for better in-laws!

Big thank you to the Portfolio team for making this book happen. Bria Sandford, without your edits this book wouldn't be worth reading. With them, I think you pushed me to my favorite book I've had the chance to work on. Margot Stamas, the reason people will know about this book is because you marketed it so well. Kaushik Viswanath, you prevented a critical Bon Jovi error from ever seeing the light of day, every author's worst nightmare.

ACKNOWLEDGMENTS

Adrian Zackheim and Will Weiser, thanks for championing the cause of authors the world over. Mike Salisbury and Curtis Yates, thanks for steering my writing career these last few years. I wouldn't dream of doing this without you guys.

Mike Peasley, your research turned this idea into a book and I will forever be grateful. Ashley Holland, the only reason I was able to turn this book in, get to speaking gigs, keep the lights on, etc., is because you're an awesome chief of staff. Thanks for your continuous support! Bryan Allain, thanks for years of hard work making sure the books don't just stay on the shelf. Thank you to everyone who took the "30 Days of Hustle" and "90 Days of Business Hustle" courses. Your feedback was invaluable. And last but certainly not least, thank you to everyone who let me use their stories in this book. You made the whole thing so much better!

NOTES

Introduction: The Wrong Ghost

3 **Angela Duckworth's excellent "Grit Scale":** Angela Duckworth.com, https://angeladuckworth.com/grit-scale/.

3 **30 Days of Hustle:** *30 Days of Hustle Summary Research Report,* compiled by Mike Peasley, University of Memphis, Department of Marketing & Supply Chain Management, 2016.

6 **Wright Brothers:** David McCullough, *The Wright Brothers* (New York: Simon & Schuster, 2015).

Chapter 1: The Day After Perfect

8 **simple breakfast of eggs:** Timothy Ferriss, *The 4-Hour Body: An Uncommon Guide to Rapid Fat-Loss, Incredible Sex, and Becoming Superhuman* (New York: Crown Archetype, 2010).

16 **"a movie of you doing":** Jack Canfield and Mark Victor Hansen, *Chicken Soup for the Soul: Unlocking the Secrets to Living Your Dreams* (New York: Simon & Schuster, 2012).

Chapter 2: Cut Your Goal in Half

21 **"planning fallacy":** Daniel Kahneman, *Thinking, Fast and Slow* (New York: Farrar, Straus and Giroux, 2013), 260.

21 **students guessed it would take:** Roger Buehler, Dale Griffin, and

NOTES

Michael Ross, "Exploring the 'Planning Fallacy': Why People Underestimate Their Task Completion Times," *Journal of Personality and Social Psychology* 67, no. 3 (1994): 366–81, web.mit.edu/curhan/www/docs/Articles/biases/67_J_Personality_and_Social_Psychology_366,_1994.pdf.

Chapter 3: Choose What to Bomb

36 **"Right now, I don't feel guilty":** J. J. McCorvey, "Shonda Rhimes' Rules of Work: Come into My Office with a Solution, Not a Problem," *Fast Company*, November 27, 2016, www.fastcompany.com/3065423/shonda-rhimes.

37 **Strategic incompetence is the act:** Josh Davis, *Two Awesome Hours: Science-Based Strategies to Harness Your Best Time and Get Your Most Important Work Done* (New York: HarperCollins, 2015), 64–65.

Chapter 4: Make It Fun if You Want It Done

49 **SMART goals . . . should be:** "SMART Goals; How to Make Your Goals Achievable," MindTools.com, www.mindtools.com/pages/article/smart-goals.htm.

56 **"It is incorrect to believe":** Daniel F. Chambliss, "The Mundanity of Excellence: An Ethnographic Report on Stratification and Olympic Swimmers," *Sociological Theory* 7, no. 1 (Spring 1989), academics.hamilton.edu/documents/themundanityofexcellence.pdf.

58 **Jeremy Cowart found a way:** See help-portrait.com.

62 **"Fear is a friend of exceptional people.":** Samuel Ha, "Top 30 Greatest Cus D'Amato Quotes," MightyFighter.com, www.mightyfighter.com/top-30-greatest-cus-damato-quotes/.

62 **As author Jonathan Fields says:** "The Truth About Motivation: Push, Pull, and Death," JonathanFields.com, www.jonathanfields.com/the-truth-about-motivation-push-pull-and-death/.

71 **"Working hard for something":** Simon Sinek, *Together Is Better: A Little Book of Inspiration* (New York: Portfolio Penguin, 2016), 105.

Chapter 5: Leave Your Hiding Places and Ignore Noble Obstacles

80 **wake up with an ironclad fist:** Bon Jovi, "Living on a Prayer," Jon Bon Jovi, Richie Sambora, and Desmond Child, on *Slippery When Wet*. Mercury, 1986, CD.

80 **Einstein did his best work:** "Career Advice from Einstein—Is This Your Miracle Year?," Escapefromcorporateamerica.com, May 19, 2009, escapefromcorporate.com/career-advice-from-einstein-genius/.

97 **The movie script became a TV show:** James Andrew Miller, *Powerhouse: The Untold Story of Hollywood's Creative Artists Agency* (New York: Custom House, 2016).

Chapter 6: Get Rid of Your Secret Rules

104 **"Cooler than Me":** Mike Posner, "Cooler than Me," Mike Posner, Eric Holljes, and Craig Klepto Tucker, RCA, 2010, digital download.

116 **Why does Will Smith believe:** www.boxofficemojo.com/people/chart/?view=Actor&id=willsmith.htm&sort=gross&order=DESC&p=.htm.

Chapter 7: Use Data to Celebrate Your Imperfect Progress

131 **"Suppose that instead of practicing":** Matthew Syed, *Black Box Thinking: Why Most People Never Learn from Their Mistakes—But Some Do* (New York: Portfolio Penguin, 2015), 46.

146 **Dan Sullivan, a well-known marketing expert:** Dan Sullivan, "Beyond the Horizon," *The Multiplier Mindset: Insights & Tips for Entrepreneurs* (blog), Strategiccoach.com, blog.strategiccoach.com/beyond-horizon/.

146 **Jeremy, the blind triathlete:** Chad Nikazy, "Why Leading a Blind Athlete Through a Triathlon Changed My Life," Trifuel.com, July 30, 2012, www.trifuel.com/training/inspiration/why-leading-a-blind-athlete-through-a-triathlon-changed-my-life.

157 **"Carpool Karaoke" segment: "Carpool Karaoke,"** *The Late Late Show with James Corden,* August 25, 2016, CBS, www.cbs.com/shows/late-late-show/video/E5E56235-8692-DE45-0309-C4BD775C807F/britney-spears-carpool-karaoke/.

159 ***Game of Thrones* author:** Chris Gayomali, "George R. R. Martin's Secret to Productive Writing: A DOS Computer" by Chris Gayomali, *Fast Company,* May 14, 2014, www.fastcompany.com/3030610/george-rr-martins-secret-to-productive-writing-a-dos-computer,

160 **Demetri Martin:** John Trowbridge, "Talking Irrelevance and 'Live (At the Time)' with Demetri Martin," *Huffington Post,* August 29 2015, www.huffingtonpost.com/entry/talking-relevance-and-live-at-this-time-with-demetri-martin_us_55e0bfb7e4b0b7a963390a5c.

NOTES

Chapter 8: The Day Before Done

172 **"Henri loves boats":** John Steinbeck, *Cannery Row* (New York: Penguin, 1992), 37.

173 **"I probably would have died:** Andy Greene, "The Last Word: Stephen King on Trump, Writing, Why Selfies Are Evil," *Rolling Stone,* June 16, 2014, www.rollingstone.com/culture/news/stephen-king-on-trump-20160609.

175 **the movie *Smokey and the Bandit*:** *Smokey and the Bandit,* directed by Hal Needham (Universal City, CA: Universal Pictures, 1977), DVD.

175 ***Cowboys & Aliens*, despite having:** *Cowboys & Aliens,* directed by Jon Favreau (Universal City, CA: Universal Pictures and DreamWorks Pictures, 2011), DVD.

178 **You're not going out there":** *Conan O'Brien Can't Stop,* directed by Rodman Flender (n.p.: Pariah, 2011).

181 **Jon Stewart made a comment:** Chris Hardwick, *The Nerdist Way: How to Reach the Next Level (In Real Life)* (New York: Berkley Books, 2011).

181 **"Every kid is one caring adult away":** Josh Shipp, "The Power of One Caring Adult," JoshShipp.com, joshshipp.com/one-caring-adult/.

Conclusion

187 ***The Voice:*** *The Voice,* directed by Alan Carter, produced by John de Mol and Mark Burnett, NBC Universal.